can be a struggle, particularly when many of us enter parenting with messages from within and without—including social media—that we are somehow not good enough, not ready, and make poor choices. Jenny Ng's book is a true lifesaver for the individual parent finding their voice of confidence. Through boldly honest reflection of her own story of parenting and gentle guidance shared with others, she offers a pathway for others."

—**Dr. Susan Walker**, Associate Professor Emeritus of Family Social Science at the University of Minnesota

"Inner child healing takes courage. Ride on Jenny's courageous self-parenting and healing journey, and take action. What do you get at the end of this courageous act? Liberation from your inner chains."

—**Janet Philbin**, licensed clinical social worker and author of the Amazon bestselling book *Show up for Yourself*

PARENTING
*un*CHAINED

Free your inner child
&
Enjoy your children

JENNY NG

LIONCREST
PUBLISHING

PARENTING UNCHAINED
Free Your Inner Child & Enjoy Your Children
First Edition

The conversations in the book all come from the author's recollections of her interactions with her family members, coaching peers, and clients, though they are not written to represent word-for-word transcripts. These memories and recollections are from the author's perspective, and she has tried to represent events as faithfully as possible. Names have been changed to protect privacy.

ISBN   978-1-5445-4055-9   *Hardcover*
       978-1-5445-4053-5   *Paperback*
       978-1-5445-4054-2   *Ebook*

To you:

*I hope this book will entice your soul to be curiously
interested in finding out what else is possible for this lifetime.*

This book is a product of living this quote:

*"Being deeply loved by someone gives you strength,
while loving someone deeply gives you courage."*
—Lao Tzu[1]

*Because of the love of Ally, I gained strength and
courage to share how I unchained my true self
through self-parenting while parenting her.*

---

1   This English quote may deviate/vary from Lao Tzu's original quote, but
      it is the quote that counts.

CONTENTS

INTRODUCTION

Joanna, a mother in her mid-forties, came to me for help because her relationship with her son had deteriorated. "Tommy won't will not talk to me anymore," she cried. She felt guilty for being a single mother, but she was also making considerable efforts to coparent her son with her ex-husband.

During her first few lessons with me, she asked about how she could be a better mother and wondered what she was doing wrong. She compared herself to other mothers and said she was not as smart or as aware as them; she was not as patient or able to control her own feelings and frustrations.

Gradually, as she put some of the tools into practice with her son, she observed some differences *inside herself*. She could look at what was happening in her inner world and watch her reactivity toward her son.

She shared with me, "I know I can do this. My relationship with my son is getting better." She stopped seeing herself as a victim and started believing that things happened *for* her, not *to* her. She believed she could create the relationship she wanted with her son by first parenting herself. Once she got to know and started to nurture her own inner child, Hidden Joanna, she came to believe she was the author of her life. That was her first taste of her awakened self, her true self.[2]

Within the next three months, she shared her ups and downs, as she was juggling her old patterns and habits and the new tools and lessons she was learning. Our bodies default to protection mode to make sure we are safe, and new tools and practices create discomfort in us. She felt pain every time she repeated her old patterns, and saw how she could not connect closer with her son. She caught her judgmental thoughts toward her son when he could not follow her desires and expectations. At times, she would do well in *honoring* the strengths of her son; however, she could not retain this positive energy as frequently as she wanted.

After five or six months of coaching sessions with me, Joanna was able to enjoy herself; she rediscovered areas she liked about herself, gained confidence, and replaced bad habits in

2   Arakelyan, "False Omniscient Personality Disorder." I have included a further explanation of the true self and false self in Chapter 1. True self is a psychological concept, also known as real self, authentic self, original self, and vulnerable self. Donald Winnicott used true self to describe a sense of self based on spontaneous authentic experience and a feeling of being alive, having a real self.

her life with good ones. She can also now observe how well she can connect with her son when she comes from a place of love and abundance.

One day, she could hardly wait to tell me about a perfect day that she and her son had shared. She was brushing her teeth and looking at a picture she had taped to the mirror: Chinese calligraphy "海阔天空" ("Boundless Sea, Vast Sky"), which described her own reflection. It reminded her of her ideal inner world: endless perception, limitless wisdom, boundless mind. It inspired her to create a delicious breakfast for her son and herself. Her son saw how hard she was working and came to help make breakfast too. Both of them had a great time that morning. Later in the day, they had heartfelt conversations where she was able to give her son space to share his thoughts without jumping in and correcting him. She also told her son that she might make mistakes at times, but she was working hard to restore her relationship with him. Her son was sitting on her lap, leaning against her body—she had missed this connection with her son so much!

Joanna still rides the emotional roller coaster from time to time. However, she is more confident that she can tap into her inner resources, go within, and connect with herself first before responding from a place of reactivity. She can accept her old patterns and befriend them. She can apply self-compassion when things are not going as planned. From a place of love and abundance, she can be a tree for her son that grows sturdier and stronger day after day, so when her son needs a tree to lean against, she can provide a place for him to rest. She knows that she will be ever ready to be there for him.

MY INNER CHILD, HIDDEN JENNY

Just as Joanna had a hidden inner child, I too always felt there was another Jenny hidden deep inside me. When I was young, I could not describe her; I did not know her well. It was a surreal feeling. I was pretty sure she was there. She had wanted to be seen and heard for a long long time. Her voice was getting louder. In my childhood, I yearned to be heard and seen, to no avail, and the yearning was still present in my adult self. Little did I know this hidden Jenny was feeling lots of pain inside me and could not show up because she was controlled by my masked outer alter ego.

I am the eldest child in my family. I have three younger sisters and one younger brother. My parents had placed high expectations on me to be a good role model for my siblings and give in to them whenever there was a conflict: who got to have the two drumsticks from the whole chicken dish, who got to brush teeth first, who got to sit in the front seat on a car ride, who got to take the remaining two ice creams, and so on.

Those days, I felt my parents were so unfair, and I interpreted that I was definitely not their favorite child because my wants and needs were not as important as what my siblings wanted and needed. Still, I was trying very hard to get attention by being a *good* girl. I did chores without my parents having

My Wounded Inner Child and My Masked Outer Alter Ego

to nag like they had to with my siblings; I earned good grades in exchange for their praise. I chose to please my parents over speaking my truth and what I truly thought. As time went by, I realized I would probably never be good enough for my parents. However, I was addicted to this thought that *Someday I will make them proud*, and I continued to carry that hope, and they disappointed me again and again.

After practicing Conscious Parenting, looking back, knowing my wounded inner child tend to be a pleaser, I realized I intentionally wanted to be a good girl to get attention and praise from my parents by getting good grades, by doing house chores, and by taking care of my siblings. However, none of these could get me any closer to receiving praise. When I was a teenager, I carried resentment, and hence, unconsciously stopped pleasing them.

This vicious cycle of having to get approval from my parents created an *I am not good enough* child inside me. It also continued until I had my own daughter and experienced her unconditional love for me. At the same time, I heard another cry for help, another inner child inside me, and I was not sure how to get her out. When I was still attending school, I was unable to look at myself in the mirror. I believed that my reflection was not me and I felt scrutinized by her.

At work, I was not able to perform to my best ability, as there was a poisonous voice telling me, *I am not good enough.*

In my marriage I could not give love or kindness to my husband; I could not even give it to myself.

In motherhood, I operated out of fear because of my not-good-enoughness. I wanted to control the outcomes of my day-to-day interaction with my daughter, to nurture my daughter's brain development so that she could grow well and be successful—successful in the way I longed to be for my own parents.

I wanted to be a "perfect" mother for my precious daughter. I wanted affirmation from my parents that not only was I a great daughter but that I could also be a great mother to their granddaughter.

With all the voices I heard inside me, I felt unsure which one was the real me. Who was I, really? Who did I want to be? Who could I become? I felt like I was everywhere and nowhere. I felt helpless, pain stricken, and confused.

MY AWAKENING JOURNEY

Not until I began telling myself, *I am enough, I am worth it because I am, I deserve better than this,* and *I am who I am, and not who I am not* did my inner voices start to change. I surrendered to whatever came to me. It was a painful process. However, it was crucial to allow me to accept myself, and later, to love myself.

Ever since I was young, I was a sensitive child and highly aware of my inner voices. I could observe how inauthentic I was when interacting with others. I would think and feel one thing but say another. I always felt that there was another "me" deep inside. I did not know who I truly was or who I was allowed to be. I only knew that I disliked who I was from the outside. At the same time, I felt helplessly under the control of my not knowing how to turn off negative self-talk. However, the turning point happened in 2010, when I realized that unconditional love is bidirectional when my baby showed me her acceptance and unconditional love. Before this moment, I had unconsciously believed I was not worthy of love. This magical touch from my baby girl was the spark of my progressive awakening journey.

· · · · · ● ● ● ● ● ● ● · · · · ·

In 1996, I became the first member of my family to go to university. Since then, I had been working in the web and digital media industry for fifteen years before I made a career switch in family life education. In 2012, I was taking a career break from long-hour and fast-paced work, spending time with my two-year-old daughter and clearing my guilt for not being there for her many "first" moments, such as her first step. She had been enrolled with a childcare center since four months old. During this career break, I was fully engaged and attended to my daughter's life. I was preparing meals for her, setting up her daily routines, being her playmate, exposing her to different activities, reflecting on my parenting styles, and thinking about what I should do next. After half a year, I decided to contribute to the growth of children and families. I enrolled myself in a master program with the University of Minnesota, Twin Cities, and earned a master of education in family education in 2017. In 2013, I launched a social enterprise called Nannies on Wheels, which provided on-demand nanny services on-the-go. I wanted to make a positive social impact by providing gainful and meaningful employment to marginalized women in the community. With our services, we brought trained nannies and purposeful play activities to children at home and met parents' needs as an alternative childcare arrangement. Since my awakening moment, I have been seeking various ways in the area of family life development.

Later, in 2014, I got introduced by June, the co-founder of my social enterprise, to attend the Landmark Forum. While taking a Landmark course, I had an aha moment: I realized I actually thought, *I do not deserve love*, and believed that about myself. I wanted to change, to believe that *I do deserve love*.

I started to listen to many different wisdom teachers whom I learned of from Oprah's OWN channels and Cal Fussman's *Big Questions* podcast: Gary Zukav, Eckhart Tolle, Dr. Shefali Tsabary, Dandapani, Thích Nhất Hạnh, Gabor Maté, Dan Siegel, and Kyle Cease, among others. These wisdom teachings helped me get out of my noisy head, the nonstop judgmental self-talks.

BECOMING A CONSCIOUS PARENTING COACH

Everyone has a different path to awakening; my path was parenting. In 2016, when I found Dr. Shefali through Oprah's show, I felt like finally someone understood what I was going through, being a mother who was still yearning for my parents' recognition. I watched her video recorded at TEDxSF and welled up with tears. I wept uncontrollably, not knowing why I had such a response. Dr. Shefali said, "Pain is the portal of transformation," and I could not agree more. Her teachings and Conscious Parenting Method helped free my trapped inner child. Since then, I have taken two yearlong courses with Dr. Shefali to become a certified Conscious Parenting Coach. I embarked on an awakening journey for myself as a woman, a mother, a daughter, a wife, an educator, and a coach. Her teachings have impacted me in so many areas of my life.

Along the journey, I saw glimpses of my wounded inner child, who felt unheard and unseen and who buried away her desire from longing for love. Through my inner child journey, I found her and felt her. I also realized at this point that to reconnect with myself, I needed to first show up with courage, face the pain, and shed my "outer protectors" layer by layer, before I could get in touch with who I really was: my authentic self. This is the spirit of wabi-sabi (Chinese: 侘寂; Japanese: 侘び寂び). With roots in Zen and the Way of Tea, wabi-sabi teaches you to see beauty in imperfection, appreciate simplicity, and accept the transient nature of all things.[3]

My intuition encouraged me to equip myself with Conscious Parenting coaching skills. In 2019, Dr. Shefali, the rest of the coaches, and I stepped into the joint movement in awakening one family at a time, getting ourselves connected with our inner selves, taking the "One Is a Million" approach, and advocating parents to raise themselves first before raising their children. We can help future generations grow into who they truly are and live their lives with less enmeshment and more freedom. This was the opportunity I wished for in the past.

CONSCIOUS PARENTING

Ever since I set off on the path of becoming a conscious parent, I gained so much by courageously facing my fear, and I gradually

---

3   Kempton, *Wabi Sabi*, 10.

regained my freedom and my deep connection with myself and obtained an empathetic and responsible relationship with my parents, my spouse, and the people around me. I can be more present now and enjoy my daughter's growing journey. Both my little Ally and I celebrated each of her developmental milestones as a preschooler, as a preteen, and now as a teenager.

I became a better mother who honors my child for who she is as we grow together along this journey. I can see how my daughter, Ally, is my spiritual partner in this lifetime. I learn a lot about myself at a deeper level through being her mother. She is far more conscious about who she is than I was at her age. She can identify the part of her that she does not enjoy being with—the part she does not feel proud of, and the other part of her that she feels is closer to who she is. In short, she is closer to her true self and has no problem to express her authenticity. Just like your children. This is a strength we as adults have lost over time. That is where our false self evolved to better operate and co-operate in society.[4]

While it takes tremendous courage, patience, and curiosity, my journey was worth the time and effort. Thanks to my growth since the end of 2016, I can now sit in front of my client, Joanna, and conduct parenting coaching sessions.

---

4   Arakelyan, "False Omniscient Personality Disorder." I have included a further explanation of the true self and false self in Chapter 1. False self is a psychological concept, also known as fake self, idealized self, superficial self, and pseudo self. "The false self...Winnicott saw as a defensive façade, which, in extreme cases could leave its holders lacking spontaneity and feeling dead and empty, behind a mere appearance of being real."

Through one coaching session after another and my workshops, I taught Joanna the possibilities of having a connection with herself and her son. She works hard to comprehend some of the tools, such as choosing to insert conscious pauses, and apply them effectively so that she can detach from her past guilt or anxiety about the future. She can choose how she wants to show up for her son, how to be with him 100 percent and connect with him in the present moment. I am committed to walk this journey with her, so that she can connect with her true self, take her power back, and experience that she is the author of her relationships.

While Joanna is still working, she can look out for the tools and resources within herself, knowing that she is responsible for making things better for herself and family.

Mila, a working mother of a school-aged girl and a preschool boy, came to me wanting to build a better relationship with her daughter but feeling helpless to do so.

Jill, a working mother of a five-year-old boy, was hardworking but wanted to do more for her son and his transition from preschool to primary school.

I too was once lost, and through parenting my child, I accessed the power of unconditional love that helped heal my inner child's wound, and I found my true self from within. Now, as a Conscious Parenting coach, I hope to connect parents through parenting and support them through the healing and awakening process.

Please note, however: if you are looking for tools as a parent for managing your children's behaviors, this may not be the book for you, as Conscious Parenting starts from raising and parenting yourself before you can parent your children from a place of love.

WHAT YOU'LL LEARN

In the darkest of storms, a lighthouse can bring lost boats back to shore. I hope I can be a lighthouse for lost families. Inspired by my own journey and training, I sat down to write this book.

Light in the Dark for Parents to Find Their Own Path Together with Their Children

This book guides you on how to connect with your inner child or true self through inner exploration such as verbal or nonverbal therapy, meditation, and journaling using your personal experiences. If an ordinary mother like me can free my inner child and enjoy my child, so can you. The more I write, the more I find there are so many directions we can dive into. I have to pause and tame my curiosity to go in all directions, so let me keep this simple with a pure heart, to give you a pure spark and get you started thinking, *Maybe there is another way to parent my child that allows me to enjoy my family life by uncovering my inner strength and love from within.*

Throughout the book, I will share my own Unchained-through-Self-Parenting process, and provide you with exercises to help you unchain your limiting belief or heal your wounded self through parenting.

MY UNCHAINED-THROUGH-SELF-PARENTING PROCESS

These exercises are called Conscious Self-Parenting and Reflection. When you come across one, I want you to put aside your protective layers—which you may be able to identify as fear-based reactions such as avoidance, controlling, resistance, numbing, skepticism, and righteousness—and simply hold these honest dialogues within you, listen with love and compassion, and pen down your responses to the questions. By taking the time to reflect on these exercises and collect your thoughts, it will help enable your Conscious Parenting and

Awareness
- Chapter 1 aims to help you recognize your true and false self.

Healing Inner Wounds
- Chapter 2 provides ways to heal your inner child or wounds.
- Chapter 3 helps you recognize your habitual patterns of dealing with emotional pain.

Conscious Observation
- Chapter 4 emphasizes practices to develop mindfulness and become a conscious observer.

Inner Being
- Chapter 5 reminds you to choose your action by inserting a conscious pause before making decisions and embodying your aliveness through the connectedness of your inner being.

SPHERIC Daily Practice
- Chapter 6 helps you sustain your change with daily practice.

Dancing with Life
- Chapter 7 gives you the CARE Method, so that you can support your child(ren) in the present moment.
- The conclusion invites you to trust your journey and live the life you want.

connect with your inner being that you may feel comfortable with or bring expansion within you. I am also hoping you gradually become a conscious observer of your thoughts and detach from "you are your thoughts." Even if they may cause pain or difficult emotions to come up, you can be self-compassionate to hold the space to contain them. Furthermore, if you are capable of self-understanding and can reflect on yourself, your skills, and your motives, you are likely to be stronger in intrapersonal intelligence.[5] You may enjoy doing Conscious Self-Parenting and Reflection. However, if this may not have been your strength, it may be a good time to start cultivating intrapersonal intelligence, also known as self-intelligence. "It is possible to develop intrapersonal intelligence through writing, mind maps, journaling, and introspection. While these activities might not appeal directly to everyone, they can be a useful way to explore the inner mind, emotions, thoughts, and feelings."[6] It is important for us as individuals, and as parents, to know more about ourselves while we are guiding and role modeling to lead others, and/or raise our children.

Before I became a conscious being and conscious parent:

- I was an insecure human being, who loved hiding behind others and yet secretly wished I could be at the center of focus.

---

5   *APA Dictionary of Psychology*, s.v., "intrapersonal intelligence."
6   Lynch, "Intrapersonal Intelligence."

- I felt unfairly treated, unacknowledged when I contributed to someone else's success.
- I unconsciously demanded the world revolve around me.
- I felt jealous of those who got more attention.
- I was hypocritical and dishonest toward myself. On the surface, I wanted to be a helpful person, but deep inside, I used my helpfulness as a means to get attention.
- I could not look at myself in the mirror because I was disgusted by my hypocritical acts.
- I longed for, but rejected or resisted, an inherent belief that I deserved love.

People Pleaser's Inferiority Complex

After I become a conscious being and conscious parent:

- I am always a curious observer of myself and a good listener for others from a place of love.
- I allow others to shine and help others succeed, unmotivated by any form of acknowledgment.
- I watch others joyfully and create conscious spaces for them to express themselves and be who they are without judgment.
- If I get emotional, I observe any misalignment within myself. I curiously hold space for Anxious Jenny, go inside, and explore what may have caused me to distance from my true self.
- I look into the mirror every day for three minutes. At first, I can hear the judgmental voices from within, but soon, I feel grateful for myself and my life.
- I can quiet my inner voices and be present with people whom I love without judging them.
- I can accept affection from others without doubting their love.

Because of my inner transformation, I can now live in a more conscious way. I can love myself first without sucking love from others like a leech. Not only can I finally free myself from the prison of my mind, but I can also share my personal growth as a humble student with natural joy. I accept that I may tumble, make mistakes, and likely repeat the same again, but I also know I can always rely on myself to bounce back and appreciate life again.

Please accept my invitation and join me to start your journey to meet your true self. By doing this one thing, you will enjoy deep connection and participation in your life and be filled with gratitude and compassion as you watch your inner child grow up.

At this point, I must also admit that walking this journey to meet your true self and live your purpose will not be easy or happen immediately. This journey requires a tremendous amount of courage and perseverance. You ought to take mistakes as learning opportunities; you will encounter countless reiterations of new discoveries and healings until you can feel grounded and closer to who you truly are.

Are you willing to take on my invitation to start living as a conscious human being? To be okay with vulnerability, the ups and downs? To practice looking inside yourself again and again until you feel grounded and love the true you? Are you committed to getting *real*? If so, getting *real* means to do the real work to get to the real you.

Along this self-parenting journey, you will get to identify your emotional pain and habitual limiting belief patterns, and see how you are the one who gets in your way to live the life you want. At the end of the day, it is to understand yourself and who you are, and enjoy your children more and your parenthood. Hopefully, you will continue to be curiously interested in raising your awareness of holistic healing. Progressively, you will come to love yourself unconditionally and willingly give space for your wounded inner child and others in your life. You will experience true love for yourself and others, as Dr. Shefali shared: "True love for the other comes with freedom, liberation; it comes without any conditions, without any hands asking for something back."

Let us begin with an end in mind now, and I will hold your hands until the day when you say this with a peaceful smile on your face: "I will take it from here."

one

WHEN MY REAL CHILD MEETS MY INNER CHILD

After seven years of marriage, I started thinking about what it would be like to become a mother.

What can I discover about myself? Am I fit for the role? Before this moment, I was too busy to consider motherhood. Studying environmental science in my first year at university, I learned that the natural resources and crops would be depleted as our populations grew. If we did not do something, humankind would be facing a crisis soon. Even with this knowledge, I still selfishly decided to become a mother and gave birth to a child. I felt an ache inside me that I could not console.

I had a confinement nanny in my first month of maternity leave. She cooked for my husband and me, helped take care of my baby when I was resting, did housework, and kept the home tidy while my husband and I transitioned into new parenthood. Zhen Jie cooked in the Chinese traditional way with herbs, lots of ginger, Chinese wine, and vinegar. That was the only period of my life where I felt like a queen. She also happened to be my mother's friend. Before she left, upon the completion of my first confinement month, my husband and I made sure that we learned all we could from her and took care of our daughter on our own thereafter.

In my second month of maternity leave, I was breastfeeding Ally in the middle of the night one night, holding her in my arms, and feeling tired. Suddenly, I felt her index finger on my cheek, a magical touch on my face. The past month, I had been feeding her, cleaning her poos, changing her diapers, pumping and storing breast milk, worrying whether she was breathing when she slept, and I was exhausting myself. However, in that moment, when she touched me, I felt my little baby girl accept everything about me, my goods and bads, my rights and wrongs, my beauty or ugliness—everything.

My own wounded inner child had been longing for love for so long and thinking, *My own parents cannot even accept me for who I am. How can anyone else?* If only I could have been smarter like other people's children, more obedient, more hardworking, more beautiful, more... I had been soaking in this "longing for love," deprived mindset. But with her magical touch, my little newborn baby gave me unconditional acceptance. She accepted me for just being there for her as a human being, not a human doing. I was not even doing that for myself. My little child connected love to my inner child, that unconditional love that my wounded inner child had been longing for.

Conscious Self-Parenting and Reflection

- Could you recall a time when you bonded well with your real child? What was the experience like? How did you feel?

- Could you also recall a time when you did not bond well with your *real* child? What hindered you from bonding with your child? How did the experience make you feel?

When she touched me, I felt a layer of my shell crack and out poured some of the pains of my not-good-enoughness. Since becoming a mother, I have become a more responsible human being than ever. Since becoming a mother, I have worked to give back to my community. The pursuit of becoming a conscious parent and conscious human being has helped me grow tremendously.

In 2010, I first met my real child, my newborn baby, Ally. I did not bond with her straightaway. In fact, I was puzzled how

I "should" feel. I found my inner world a little too cold. As I recalled from the movies or dramas I watched, parents always receive their newborn baby with pure joy and happy tears. I was, in fact, searching hard for some emotions inside of me, but they were empty. I whispered and said hello to baby Ally when the nurse placed her in the hospital crib next to me. Shortly after the completion of newborn screening tests, the nurse placed her on my chest and encouraged us to bond through breastfeeding. With the up close and personal skin-to-skin contact, my icy cold internal world finally melted.

Conscious Self-Parenting and Reflection

- When (if at all) did you start feeling a bond with your *inner child*? As you journey through self-acceptance, watch how that bond strengthens.
- Recall a time (if any) when you felt unconditional acceptance. What was it like?
- If you have yet to bond with your inner child, start with lowering the volume of your negative self-talk within. What are some examples of negative self-talk to tune out?
- How would you describe some ways you love your inner child? Do they operate from a place of fear (e.g., wanting to control others or your real child[ren], and things around them, to calm your fear down), or from the place of love (e.g., accepting the sovereignty of others or your child[ren])?

Between 2010 and 2016, there were up and down moments being a mother. I knew there was much guilt because it was not easy to balance work life and family life, and I had to send her to an infant care center when she was four months old. In 2010, during Ally's first year, becoming a mother was life-changing for me. Though I felt my melted heart from within through skin-to-skin contact, and the magical touch from my little Ally during breastfeeding time, I still felt defeated at times. Even though I enjoyed my time with Ally, and tried to spend "productive" and "meaningful" time with her through purposeful play, the emptiness from within still visited me when I was vulnerable. Looking back, I now realize I was trying so hard to be a good mother because of my lack that came from my childhood wounds. There was "another me" that got in my way. I got to experience that wounded child from within during Inner Child Visualization meditation in 2017. As Thích Nhất Hạnh described in the section "The Child Within" in his book *Reconciliation: Healing the Inner Child*:

> In each of us, there is a young, suffering child. We have all had times of difficulty as children and many of us have experienced trauma. To protect and defend ourselves against future suffering, we often try to forget those painful times. Every time we're in touch with the experience of suffering, we believe we can't bear it, and we stuff our feelings and memories deep down in our unconscious mind. It may be that we haven't dared to face this child for many decades. But just because we

may have ignored the child doesn't mean she or he isn't there. The wounded child is always there, trying to get our attention.[1]

From 2017, as I began to heal my wounded inner child, I got to shed some of my false selves or egoic selves, who were trying to protect me from feeling pain, or to "prove" I was worthy of love. Along the healing process, as I accepted who I was and the imperfect me, I shed more protective layers, which were my false selves. My true self was curling within, waiting for me to come to its rescue—waiting for me to see, hear, and feel it within. There are many paths and ways to uncover and heal your inner child. I am going to share with you some of the methods, approaches, and tools I have experienced to heal my childhood wounds in Chapter 2.

I hope through this book and my invitation, you can start being curious about healing your inner child, and subsequently, this self-parenting journey will bring you closer to your children and help you enjoy your growing journey together.

MEETING MY TRUE SELF

Let us begin by defining true self and false self. The psychological theory of the true and the false self comes from one of the twentieth century's greatest thinkers, the English psychoanalyst and child psychiatrist Donald Woods Winnicott.

---

1   Hạnh, *Reconciliation*, 4.

According to Winnicott, the false self has an important function: to hide the true self, which it does by compliance with environmental demands. The false self may emerge when a child enters school, for instance. In school, children learn how to be polite and behave in a socially acceptable way. At home, children learn to show only what parents want to see, and become someone that they are not. Winnicott added, a healthy false self is necessary and desirable for us to exist in the world, as it enables us to be polite and comply with rules and regulations, even when we do not want to. However, when the false self is a defensive facade, behind which the person can feel empty, its behaviors are learned and controlled rather than spontaneous and genuine. This false self is inauthentic because its spontaneous desires are hidden away. He or she has learned to comply far too early and to become obedient at the expense of his or her ability to feel authentically.[2]

The true self comes from the aliveness of body tissues and the working of bodily functions, including automatic functions like breathing, blinking, and pumping blood. The true self is closely linked with the Primary Process and is, at the beginning, essentially not reactive to external stimuli. There is little function in formulating a true self except for the purpose of trying to understand the false self because it does no more than collect together the details of the experience of aliveness. To further elaborate, the true self feels real through the feeling of

2   McKeever, "True or False."

existing and living in the body itself; at the same time, the true self senses genuine doing through creativity and with autonomy.[3] In contrast, when the true self feels real, the existence of the false self results in a feeling unreal or a sense of futility.[4]

Another term used for true self is "inner child," as Alice Miller, psychotherapist, describes it. Dr. Charles Whitfield, a physician and psychotherapist, defines "inner child" as an "ultimately alive, energetic, receptive, creative, and fulfilled" part of our psyche.[5] "When this part of us is not nurtured and allowed expression and the inner child is denied, a 'false self' or persona emerges. This self denies or hides feelings, is fearful, constantly planning and controlling. It is critical, perfectionistic, rational, other-oriented, and overly confirming."[6] With safe therapeutic help, the notion of being "true to ourselves" becomes much clearer and more meaningful, and we can move toward a healthy understanding of who we are while finding the contentment and genuine connection to reality missing from our lives.[7]

I first met my true self in 2017, when I embarked on my awakening journey. A coursemate of ours in the Year of Awakened Heart shared her Inner Child Visualization audio with us to listen to later on our own. In the middle of the night, I did that visualization, and these internal dialogues followed:

---

3   Alfaya, "Response to the Editorial."
4   Winnicott, "Ego Distortion."
5   Whitfield, *Healing the Child Within*, 1.
6   Grossberg, "Let Your Inner Child Dance," 51.
7   McKeever, "True or False."

My adult self said to my inner child, who was wounded during childhood, *It is okay; everything is going to be alright. I will hold your hand and walk this life with you without letting go. It is okay; I am here.*

My adult self opened my (inner child's) heart up with a sense of security and eased my fear. My adult self lovingly said, *Inner child, you can step out of the "dungeon" now. Come fly with me; experience the sky and the world with me.*[8]

My wounded inner child had been waiting for someone to show up and set her free. For so long, there were no signs that any heroes would come to the rescue—because I was looking for rescue from outside.

Now that I have realized I am my own hero, I can connect with my true self deeply, speak from a place of love, and act without people-pleasing motivations. I felt my mind, body, and heart join and center. I felt real and like I no longer needed to hide. Though my false self still functions within social context (where I need to comply with social rules, spoken or unspoken, in order to better connect with others), I can now constantly align and realign myself with my purpose. I know when I am out of alignment and take time and space to bring myself back to my center, my compassionate heart. My false self is no longer my enemy because I can now see it as a way to protect my true self, a way to get my practical needs and wants met.

---

8   Redden, "Guided Inner Child Visualisation."

Additionally, through the practice of meditation, I can observe my decisions and determine whether they were made from a place of love or fear.

Conscious Self-Parenting and Reflection

- Describe a time you felt lost, when you were disgusted or disappointed with yourself. How did you pick yourself up and recover from that disappointment?
- Have you discovered your inner truth? What do you believe it is? How did you come to connect with it?

It takes lots of practice and hard work to uncover your true self. When I was first awakened:

- I wanted to live nonnegotiably.
- I wanted to do something good for others.
- I recognized and accepted my strengths and abilities.
- I started to look into growing myself and expanding my potential.

The light within me ignited and energized me from within. After my shell cracked, after I connected with my true self, I could express kindness toward myself. Here is what I wrote down in my journal:

I am kind.
I am honest.
I am curious.
I am playful.
I am here to bring parents to their full consciousness to parent their inner child.
I am here to remind parents to give space to their child(ren) to grow into their true selves.
I am here to provide parents tools to bring their parent–child relationship closer than ever.
I am whole. I am home. I am worth it.
I am enough because I am.

I will keep these small candles of hope lit inside my heart, even when there is wind, even when people want to blow out their flames. I will protect this light in me and show others the light inside themselves too. Together, our lights will pierce the darkness, so we can all discover the treasure within ourselves and live our truths.

EFFECTIVE AFFIRMATIONS

Life was less content until I took two yearlong courses with Dr. Shefali Tsabary from 2016 to 2018. From 2016 to 2017, I took part in Dr. Shefali's first yearlong course, "The Year of Awakened Heart," and for the first time, I saw what a mess my life was. I started letting go of who I could not be and accepted who I am and always have been. I learned that I was only a failure in my own mind; the version of myself I strove to be was an illusion. I started embracing the whole me and courageously accepting who I was and who I was not. When I felt that I was whole and complete, there were fewer judging voices that kept repeating who I had to be or had not become. I felt tons of stone in my mind being relieved. From then on, I could just be myself and discover and acknowledge who I am. I am unique like everyone else, and everyone else is unique like me.

From 2017 to 2018, not only could I be myself, having the qualities that make me who I am, I could also see my life beyond myself, how my life also contributes to others. Since my awakening journey, I am becoming one with the universe on a spiritual level.

This is what I have found in my journal for the shift:

I am enough.

I am bold.

I am courageous.

I am anything and everything (no self-limitation).

I am bigger than myself.

I hold positive feelings about myself.

I hold positive feelings about others.

I am them; they are me.

We are oneness in the entire universe.

I managed to overcome my pain by revealing my true self through the daily practice of Conscious Parenting. I am very grateful to Dr. Shefali for showing up as who she is and teaching parents like me to honor their children.

By awakening and meeting my true self, I continually reap these benefits:

- I get to fully live my life, in all its brightness or gloom.
- I get to discover equanimity.
- I get to experience full gratitude.
- I get to touch my own heart in a deep way.
- I get to know the reason my heart is touched.
- I get to challenge myself to reach the unimaginable future.

MOVING ALONG MY AWAKENING JOURNEY

On an ordinary day, I wake up at six in the morning and proceed with my morning rituals. I meditate and practice Wu Tao Dance Therapy.[9] There are times when I just want to sit in front of the TV and keep my thoughts busy, engrossed with external stimulations so that I do not have to process them, but I fight those urges because I know what my daily practice has brought to my life.

I start working with calmness from within and simply observe my emotional state. Because I start my morning with

---

9   Wu Tao Dance Therapy founded by Michelle Locke, an Australian ballet dancer, therapist, and registered nurse.

this mindset, I am better able to observe my emotions throughout the day. From there, I can usually pause and decide my next
step(s). During times when pausing is more difficult, when I
am triggered or overtaken by reactivity, I choose to hold space
for these emotional reactions, be compassionate with myself,
and breathe through my reactions to regulate my nervous system. Sometimes, if I am not in a place to do my breathing technique, I do reflective journaling.

Conscious Self-Parenting and Reflection

If you have not started meditation,
and you are not familiar with
observing from within—your inner
world, such as your emotional state—
you may start by experiencing
looking at yourself in the mirror,
observing yourself from outside in.

Observing Yourself in the Mirror
Connect with yourself through looking at yourself in the
mirror for three minutes. Feel free to adjust and extend the
duration if you prefer a longer exercise.

1. Set a three-minute timer.
2. Close your eyes. Take three deep breaths and when
   you are ready, tell yourself silently, "I am ready to begin."
   Then, open your eyes.
3. As you open your eyes, what do you first notice? Make
   a mental note.

4. Slowly, pay attention to your whole face and notice your blinks.

5. Look at your eyebrows, eyes, nose, lips, cheeks, ears, and your facial features.

6. Gently, pay attention to your facial muscles. Sense and feel them. Are they relaxed or tight?

7. In between, you may take a few deep breaths to bring yourself back to where you are, and to the present moment; you may also take a mental note on what distracts you, or what makes you drift away.

8. You may observe other parts of your body in the mirror, depending on what you can see in the mirror.

9. Slowly and gently, transition to mindful listening, and listen to your thoughts; if you like, make a mental note about your thoughts.

10. You may repeat and observe different parts from your body to your mind, or from your mind to your body.

11. You may gaze at one part (e.g., connect with yourself through looking into your eyes) until the timer is up.

You may jot down the mental notes in your journal, reflect, and/or integrate what you have discovered about yourself from this exercise. On the scale of 0 to 5, choose how comfortable you were in connecting with yourself in the mirror:

- Scale 0: I am very distracted by my judgmental thoughts or voices; there is no single quiet moment at all.
- Scale 5: I am able to follow the flow of observing myself moment by moment. I hear no judgmental voices or thoughts in my head; I am very comfortable with myself watching myself from the outside in.

If you have rated yourself at scale 2 or below, it is good feedback and an invitation for you to consider scheduling breathing meditation sessions in a regular manner. If you have rated yourself at scale 3 or above, you may be a beginner conscious observer; if not, you are working toward becoming a solid mindfulness practitioner. Keep up the good work in practicing mindfulness! If you have not integrated mindfulness in your parenting journey, I hope this book gives you ideas to connect and apply during your daily interaction with your child(ren).

Daily practice has helped me grow in all dimensions along this journey. Daily communion with myself grants me the expansive space to learn through my mistakes and better connect with my loved ones, friends, and new people. Without first acknowledging my imperfections, I cannot accept my beautiful, unique self just the way I am.

Here are the positive side effects of getting to know my true self:

- I now speak from my inner truth with compassion. I do not say what I think others want to hear. I know there is nothing for me to protect myself from or fight against. Thích Nhất Hạnh suggests compassionate listening or deep listening and has four mantras for reducing suffering (see "My Go-To Wisdom Teachers"). During difficult times, I use these for quieting my negative self-talk too, or I recite aloud to my daughter and let her know I have got her back. From my observation on how she received these mantras, she did not appreciate them every time. However, at times, as I recited with different tonality, it helped her break her negativity state and burst into laughter.

- Because I am deeply connected with who I truly am, I can also get connected to the *why* of my existence. I pay attention to what I can offer to people around me, or to the world.

- I know where I stand with my boundaries. When I am treated beyond what I am willing to accept, I know I have the power to stand up for myself.

- When I am lost, I feel no stress because I hold the space for myself. I listen for the answer to surface from inside out.

- Through awareness and growth, I get to meet people who are also curiously interested in personal growth, or rather my compassionate self is able to connect with people around me better as I connect with their inner desire to grow.

Though our false selves try to protect us from a place of fear, our daily practices will help us be compassionate, even in our responses to our false selves. Looking back, having understood the function of false self, my younger self sacrificed my authenticity in exchange for connection and love. Today, I am showing up here and now with my authenticity, hoping my journey can spark your curiosity and courage in getting to know your authentic self.

When my daughter touched my face and showed me true acceptance, I realized unconditional love was bidirectional, parents to child and child to parents. My girl, who is now twelve years old, loves me with all her heart and accepts me unconditionally for who I am. I knew, then and there, that I needed to rescue myself. No one else could do this for me. The hero I was looking for was always in me—and it is in you too.

two

HEAL YOURSELF A LITTLE EACH DAY

T he healing journey starts from discovering your emotional pain, or to be more precise, it starts from an inner child wound, where it is the cause of your emotional pain. This unresolved emotional pain may be long forgotten, or you may be feeling the pain from the wound right now. In this chapter, I hope to share some effective healing methods I experienced personally.

WHERE MY HEALING JOURNEY BEGAN

My healing journey only began after I could fully accept myself. Additionally, the realization of self-acceptance helped me to see the hindrance of me feeling worthy was my self-judgmental thoughts (e.g., *I need to do or know more, then I will be worthy of love and attention when I achieve success*, or *I can become the perfect person who knows it all*). Having awareness and self-acceptance, I became curious about ways to heal my wounded inner child. There is a fine line between these two thoughts: (1) I need to achieve and do more to get to another peak—deep down, one might have a deeper desire to prove his or her worth; (2) I am worthy for who I am; I have freedom to choose and create a fulfilling life. Can you accept who you are just by being you at this very moment? If not, what would stop you from accepting who you are just by being you? Take a ride with me to have a peep of your own possible healing journey.

From "I Do Not Deserve Love" to "I Am Enough"

I was a sensitive child. My needs went unmet, unacknowledged, unrecognized, and unheard. I felt abandoned and betrayed. In my childhood, I "locked" myself up in a "safe place" (my comfort zone), so no one could disappoint me again—so that I could not feel pain or sadness or, really, anything again. Not even hope. I avoided self-disclosure to the outside world.

My mother considered me stubborn. She said I always made mean comments when she talked to me. As I recalled and reflected upon my childhood, I discovered that I did not believe my parents loved me because, deep down, I had this belief that I did not deserve love.

Of course, it was my own interpretation of their love through my own lenses, based on our daily interactions when I was growing up: the way my mother scolded me when she wanted me to help out around the house, the way my father wanted me to give in to my younger siblings because I was the eldest, the pressure I put on myself to perform well in my studies to please my parents. I could now see that what they said or did was for my own good. However, in childhood, I believed that they only wanted me to help them look good, and I interpreted their actions as fake love. Looking back, I realize that that interpretation was a projection of me—my false self. I thought that I was not worth their love and I could never satisfy their expectations of me. This was where *People-Pleasing Jenny* was born, one of my personalities mentioned in Chapter 3.

When I was in my mid-thirties, I found myself suffocated by this fake person, my false self. I forced myself to conform to societal expectations, such as hanging out with coworkers so that I would not be called antisocial, and agreeing with what everyone else said even though I had a different viewpoint, so that I could blend in well. I had no boundaries for myself at all, I would not let my voice be heard, and I hated that about myself. Even then, I could feel there was another me deep inside that yearned to get out.

Before I began my healing journey, I thought life was happening *to* me, not *for* me. I thought it was my siblings' fault that my parents could not love me the way I needed. I kept changing jobs because I believed, over and over, that I did not have bosses with strong leadership skills; or when bosses with strong leadership skills left the company, I left with them. I was married to my husband only because he chose me to be his wife, and I did not say no. I was playing "victim" in my head. I was not proud of who I had become, but I did not know how to release my "true self" trapped inside me (neither did I know who I was, nor was I my true self back then). I was hoping to release my true self, so that I could escape from being fully controlled by false self, who cares about looking good in front of others and suppressing my true self's needs. False self has its own function to keep us safe, comply with social rules, and play a part in contributing to the workplace, school, and society as a whole.

UNDERSTANDING MY PARENTS

After raising my consciousness levels, I have discovered that I am the cocreator of everything that happens in my life. Looking back, I can understand why my parents raised me differently from their other five children. I can also have compassion for my parents, who did not know better due to how they were parented.

My maternal grandmother passed away when my mother was a teenager. Since then, my mother has been very close to her siblings. When she was seventeen, she decided to leave her hometown of Johor, Malaysia, and her siblings, for Hong Kong, so that she could pick up a skill or two to make a living. She then went back to Malaysia, married my father, and became a business owner as a tailor and a hairdresser in Johor Bahru, the capital city of Johor in Malaysia. I can still vaguely recall that a few certificates my mother received from Hong Kong were hung on the wall of her hair salon-cum-boutique shop, a business that acts as both a hair salon and tailor. My younger sister and I were running around while she was serving her customers. She was doing haircuts at one moment, and the next moment, she was taking measurements on her customers who came for tailoring of their clothes. As we were chatting about the past, she said, "I do not know much about raising children. The only thing I knew back then was that it was my responsibility as a woman to give birth to children, work, and earn enough to live life."

During my teenage years, my mother's loud nagging voice would linger in my ears. I remember her saying, "Go do your homework!" "Have you helped clean up?" and our names would be called repeatedly. My siblings and I would sulk and do what we were told. Along this awakening journey, as I healed my inner wounds—many of them were from my own interpretation of my parents' love for me, especially those that made me feel unworthy when I was not seen or heard, and feel that my needs were not important—I saw my parents were just raising us in the best possible way they knew. They just repeated patterns of how they were raised. A great sense of empathy and gratitude filled me, and even though the beginning of my awakening journey seemed challenging with some egoic voices wanting to justify what was right or wrong, that wounded child was having mixed feelings. Now, I am able to be compassionate with myself and my mother, who did not know better when she was raising us. As I self-parent my inner child, the uncertainty and self-righteousness is resolved with love and kindness.

My father was the fourth son out of eleven children from my paternal grandparents. He had to help my grandmother collect rubber at the rubber plantation "...in the early morning before the day's temperature rose, so the latex would drip longer before coagulating and sealing the cut."[1] He shared some of his childhood memories with us, telling us that breakfast was limited and only available for the "early birds." If you were late in waking up, you would still need to go to work with an empty stomach.

To him, education is very important, as he did not have the privilege to finish his primary or elementary school, and priorities were given to some of his siblings. Hence, as a father, he was committed to providing educational opportunities to all five of us when we were young, so that we could increase our chances to have better lives than both of our parents. He started his building construction company from scratch when I was young, and now one of my siblings is a partner of the business. I was certainly eager to achieve similar success, and I finally accepted I was not who I thought I could be.

My father once told me, "It would not be possible to interact with your youngest sister the same way I do with your third sister." I did not understand what he shared with me then, but now, I know he was right. My third sister was a more cautious

---

1   Prasad, "Rubber Tapping Machine."

and quiet child when she was young. My youngest sister, in contrast, was loud and bold, confronting people she did not like. Both my father and my youngest sister can joke around with one another. When my father is with my third sister, however, they communicate calmly and politely and engage in sincere conversations. I had to first acknowledge the uniqueness in each and every one of us before I could understand that my mother and father parented me the way they did out of love.

As for my job hopping, that had nothing to do with the skills of other people. It was more due to my self-limiting beliefs and lack of self-confidence and trust in myself. Yes, I also wanted to prove to my parents I could meet their expectations of me— which was my own interpretation of their expectations—that I was enough and worthy of their love.

Conscious Self-Parenting and Reflection

- Describe your relationship with your parents. Rate your relationship on the scale of 0 to 5, where 0 equals "We no longer have a relationship" and 5 equals "We talk to one another regularly, about anything and everything." If the rating is not 5, what do you think is missing in your relationship?
- Did anything happen during your childhood that created limiting beliefs (e.g., *I do not deserve love*)?

Comparison with Others Is a Vicious Cycle

Before I started my path of awakening, one of my biggest pains in life was that I could never live up to my parents' expectations, especially if they would constantly compare me with other people's children. To them, success meant wealth, beauty, expensive possessions, and status symbols, a lavish lifestyle. My dad and his siblings love to compare who is doing better—who has the bigger house, the more expensive car, smarter kids, etc. I conformed to those expectations, and I was hoping to be seen and heard by my parents, by anyone. Slowly and unknowingly, I buried my authenticity and became inauthentic in an effort to gain "love" and connection from my parents and the people around me.

I used to feel like a loser around them, especially when I decided to quit my job and set up a social enterprise to help others. Having received unconditional love from my daughter, my love tank was filled. I felt like I had the power to do anything I wished to do, and I wanted to make a difference for children. I wished to provide children opportunities to see the goodness in themselves: strengths, talents, natural abilities to create, etc. to allow them to grow into who they are (natural abilities) and who they can be. It was a mirror from my inner battle when I was younger: I wished I could grow into who I was, not who I wished to be, or who I thought my parents or people around me wanted me to be. I did not have the space to be seen as who I really was, nor to speak what I really wanted to say from the bottom of my heart (and be heard). I felt like my deep-asleep me awakened and was ready to start something meaningful for children. At least, that is what I wished I could have had when I was a child.

PURSUING MY PASSION, NOT PERCEIVED SUCCESS DEFINED BY OTHERS

As my wounded inner child is healed a little each day, I can observe how I have progressed from self-acceptance to self-compassion little by little. My longing for love and affirmation from outside or from my parents is diminishing too. I have been letting go of pursuing the perceived successful life defined by others and giving myself the permission and freedom to pursue my passion. In 2012, I quit my full-time employment with a digital agency. I decided to set up a social enterprise where I could take mobile nanny services to homes. I hoped to train nannies and provide them jobs, so that they could engage children with meaningful and purposeful activities while taking care of them at home. This idea was inspired from my childhood and one of my English literature reading materials, *Mary Poppins*; later while taking an English literature course, I watched the movie. I hoped our nannies would bring "magical moments" to children too. I then formalized it as a business entity. This social enterprise was first named Family Tales Pte. Ltd., and then Nannies on Wheels LLP. We first recruited single mothers, retirees, mothers with empty-nest syndromes, and stay-at-home mothers. In 2013, my partner, June Tangsakul, came on board, and we tried to grow this business together. We had some precious moments together with our team of twenty-ish, bringing children for outdoor learning, looking after children at their homes, building good relationships with parents, and reporting our childrens' healthy growth. To sustain the business, we needed to have more engagement from parents, and we needed to recruit more nannies to provide the services. While the Nannies on Wheels administrative team earned SGD5 per hour from the SGD25 per hour we charged parents, and the rest of the money went to nannies, it could still be a high price for parents to be able to afford our services. We were trying to meet up with some government agencies to further support, such as providing subsidies for parents to engage in our services. However, there was no progress after a few rounds of discussions. I think we got stuck because of the very same reason: both sides wanted to make sure children were safe and healthy. The business was set up because we wanted children to have purposeful care sessions with our nannies and enjoy healthy growth and at the same time, to enable a safe and healthy environment (their own home) for sick children. Government agencies did not make progress because they wanted to make sure children would be safe and healthy under our care.

I was not making much money then. I had to work part-time as a lecturer to support myself. My business partner, June, and I sustained the business till 2021. Then, we ceased operations and closed the last chapter of our social enterprise.

While I was running Nannies on Wheels, I was also completing my master of education in family education, pursuing my passion in helping parents, and spreading the concept of Conscious Parenting. I gained so much after becoming a conscious mother and coach, I have found my authentic self and true voice from within. I reclaimed my power. I can choose to live my life differently. I can relive, and it is not over yet.

Being a more conscious human now, I am breaking hard out of my old patterns. Here I am, standing firm to set up another business as a parenting coach. Since 2020, I have gained some traction from Chinese-speaking mothers around the globe, sharing how I was unchained via my parenting journey, and how I continue to sustain my life energy to live the way I want my life to be.

Though my father did not tell me outright, he was angry with me when I told him that I was quitting my full-time job as a program manager in February 2020, at the beginning of the COVID-19 pandemic. After that day, whenever he spoke to me, he responded in anger. As an observer and deep listener since my awakening journey, I could identify that, in fact, he was upset with my decision to quit my stable job.

The day I had this realization, I called him up and said this:

"Dad, I know you are upset with my decision to let go of a stable income to start my own business as a Conscious Parenting coach. You see success as owning money and possessions, but I view it as making a meaningful contribution to society. Grandma used to hold both of my hands and pray in front of the Buddha, wishing for me to grow into someone useful. My interpretation of usefulness is helping others. I hope to help people by teaching them to consciously parent themselves before, or while, raising their own children. I believe this will help more children be seen and heard. They can find their own successes in life and overcome any future challenges. I want to thank you and Mom for bringing me up the way you did. I know both of you did your best for me. You generously sponsored my university study, which gave me the opportunities to work in the information technology industry for fifteen years. That was also part of me; it helped me grow into who I am today. Thank you, Dad."

When I finished, my mother, who had been listening to our conversation, commented aloud, "Dad is tearing up." As soon as I heard that, I could not hold my tears any longer.

I loved my dad and mom enough that day to show them my true self, whom I had been searching for half of my life. I am so grateful they had the chance to meet the real me in this lifetime. All the work was worth it.

I still feel self-doubt sometimes, but I hold space for myself, and the universe holds space for me too. My mind and body are in alignment, and I believe my newfound truth has given me the courage and curiosity to engage fully in this game of life. When I do not have the answer, I just have to trust that I am moving toward my purpose, and I do not look back.

Conscious Self-Parenting and Reflection

- "It takes courage to show your true self." Can you relate to this? What happened?
- Have you accepted who you truly are, and worked not to become who you think others want you to be? Was the acceptance process a challenging one? Why?

You Are Not Your Thoughts

I felt a great sense of freedom the moment I realized *I do not deserve love* was a limiting belief, but I still did not believe in my spirit that I was worthy of love. It was difficult for me to separate myself from my habitual limiting beliefs, my thoughts.

Through Dr. Shefali's online meditation courses, I started practicing Vipassana meditation (or insight meditation), a breathing technique (also mentioned in the "Meditation" section) that enables the meditator to detach and observe his or her thoughts. Close your eyes, focus on your usual breathing. Pay attention to each inhale and exhale; observe your thoughts, feelings, and sensations without reacting or judging. When time is the constraint, you can also practice this breathing technique with open eyes, focus on your usual breathing, and pay attention to each inhale and exhale while doing household chores, cooking, watering plants, etc. If you become distracted, simply acknowledge you are distracted and return to your breath.

As you practice this meditation over time, you realize sooner or later your thoughts are your thoughts, and your thoughts are not you. You do have the choice if you would like to interfere with your thoughts, such as you detach and watch your thoughts from a distance, or engage in a thought. As you strengthen your mindfulness muscles, you may also notice your negative or positive thoughts, and that, for the negative ones, you do not have to succumb to reactivity like I once did. To avoid overthinking, "instead of giving more attention to your thinking, you take your attention into the inner energy of your body, and suddenly, you feel the aliveness that pervades the entire body. You have retaken consciousness away from the mind," as Eckhart Tolle explained consciousness.[2] To avoid unconsciously spiraling into your thoughts, it would be good to redirect your awareness to the inner energy of your body and allow the sense of energy flow to remind you of your being and your aliveness. It is a good reminder that you are not your thoughts, and to avoid overthinking.

To further deconstruct the mind and its relationship with energy, Dr. Dan Siegel, author of *Mindsight: The New Science of Personal Transformation*, defined the mind "as an emergent, self-organizing process that arises from, and also regulates

---

2   Tolle, "Eckhart Tolle Special Live Teaching."

energy and information flow within the brain and within relationships with others." He further elaborated in a recorded interview titled "What Makes a Healthy Mind" with Tami Simon, the founder of Sounds True: "Energy, in the physics terms of energy, like you need energy to have a thought, you need energy to turn on a light bulb or move your arm, literal energy. And information is an experience where we symbolize things as representing something other than they are. For example, the word rock is information for the stone in your hand. It is not the stone itself. So this flow of energy and information describes a mental experience. But the regulation of it is a very important aspect of the mind." In this particular interview, Dr. Dan Siegel explained that the healthy mind consists of two foundations of regulation.

Monitoring or observing. Often people do not observe or monitor their own mind, which can be described as a kind of mind blindness. This results in people being impulsive and reactive, saying things that are unkind, or even doing things that are destructive. However, when you have learned to monitor energy and information flow, you can then take the pulse of where your life has rigidity in it. When you have repeated habits that you feel imprisoned by or thoughts that keep on going over and over in your head, that is an example of rigidity.

Now the good thing about the mind is, almost everyone can be assisted in developing the skills to see more deeply into their energy and information flow, to have mindsight, to actually see and shape the inner flow that is their subjective inner world. They can actually become an active author of their own story. That can see their own mind and actually see the mind of others.

Modifying. With the developed skills to see the energy and information flow, we can choose to shape the inner flow of our subjective inner world. For instance, with kindness and compassion toward myself and others, I can move into a different kind of space or experience where I just accept things as they are. This is obviously an ancient teaching in mindfulness practice, to have this curiosity, openness, and acceptance, which is in many ways the basis of love. A healthy mind now is one that is not stuck in chaos, rigidity or both, but actually is coming into a place of flexibility and adaptability or a sense of coherence, which subjectively feels like harmony.[3]

In Dr. Dan Siegel's definition, consciousness, subjective experience, and information processing are the three parts of the mind.

Linking back to mindfulness practice, the breathing technique, which I practiced through meditation sessions led by Dr. Shefali Tsabary over two years, presented a paradigm shift for me in my communication style and my relationships. As I become an observer of my thoughts, I can then modify energy and information flow, and I insert a conscious pause before

3   Siegel, "What Makes a Healthy Mind."

responding. This conscious pause allows me to make a conscious choice of options I have, before I take my values-based action (Chapter 4). My interaction with my daughter, Ally, has shifted from reactive to responsive, and I am better able to listen to her needs and support her without internalizing her behaviors. In other words, I learned to be responsible for my own emotions and let my child be responsible for hers.

Whatever happens externally is a projection of my inner world. If Ally refuses to follow my instructions, an external response, I feel rejected internally. The more I want to control my fear of being rejected, the more likely I am to shout at her for not listening to me. My desire to control something that is outside of me points to a weakness in myself. It comes from a place of fear and lack. However, when I pause and choose my response as an observer, instead of allowing the fear to take over, I can respond to my child by attuning to her and listening to her needs at that moment.

I am who I am today, as I am grateful for uncovering my authentic truth and having the courage to break the old patterns, one after another, all thanks to my curiosity. It gives me hope through experiencing a little healing one after another. Yes, you may hesitate and point out that "curiosity killed the cat," but do give some space to the curious you—leave this option open, muster up your courage to continue to connect with your inner terrain, learn more about yourself and possible healing methods when needed—because "satisfaction brought it (the cat) back."

EFFECTIVE METHODS FOR HEALING

There are many ways to heal or connect with your inner child. Here are some effective methods and approaches I have used to heal my childhood wounds over time, and now I use them to help my clients heal.

The Conscious Parenting Method by Dr. Shefali

What is Conscious Parenting?

If you happen to have read one of the parenting books written by Dr. Shefali, *The Conscious Parent: Transforming Ourselves, Empowering Our Children*, you would have found this description of Conscious Parenting:

> An innovative parenting style recognizes the child's potential to spark a deep soul-searching, leading to transformation in parents. Instead of being merely the receiver of the parents' psychological and spiritual legacy, children function as ushers of the parents' development. In short, children serve as mirrors of the parents' forgotten self. Once a parent finds their way back to their essence, they enter into communion with their children. Parent and child awaken to the ability to relate in a state of presence.[4]

---

4   Tsabary, *The Conscious Parent*.

In upcoming chapters, you will find more stories and lessons I learned from my interactions with my daughter. I will share how parents may have raised their level of consciousness through Conscious Parenting.

First, I would invite you to observe and notice an area where you tend to control your child most is also where your greatest fear is. For example, I used to control how my daughter spent her play time when she was still a toddler. I would make sure I engaged her with planned activities. These activities would have to be fun, purposeful, and educational. I thought, *I ought to stimulate Ally's brain development as early as possible, so that she can be smarter, wiser, and happier when she grows up*. Neither did I know nor did I understand that it was due to my childhood wound of being teased because I could not answer questions people whom I respected or loved asked me. It was painful deep inside me that my inner child was avoiding revealing my "not good enoughness." I hoped to see my daughter become smarter, wiser, and happier than I could when I was younger. The Conscious Parenting Method helped me first to be aware of my wounds by sharing my unpleasant interaction with my child with my peer, who was also in the process to get certified as a Conscious Coaching Institute coach in the first cohort of Dr. Shefali's Coaching Institute.

During the session, we as coaches will explore old patterns and recent concerned behaviors clients have. Depending on the clients' needs and readiness, Conscious Parenting coaches may be able to have the client recall and connect to a childhood incident that happened, and help the client understand how his or her emotional baggage is linked to the unhealed wound.

In this chapter, I will also share different ways to heal childhood wounds that I experienced before. Additionally, I will explain how practicing mindfulness can help you consistently be more mindful of your internal world and habitual limiting belief patterns. You will also be curious about where your emotional reactivities come from, and you will make conscious choices to respond to your child's behaviors instead of reacting to them. As you are more aware of how your own thoughts, feelings, and behaviors are affecting your reactivity or unconscious choice of action due to your own childhood experiences, you will get to practice making conscious choices by deconstructing your thoughts, feelings, and behaviors using guides and tools provided in Chapters 4 and 5.

The Compassionate Inquiry by Dr. Gabor Maté

I experienced the Compassionate Inquiry approach when I attended Dr. Gabor Maté's Compassionate Inquiry Self-Study Short Course.

This description of the approach comes from the course materials:

> The purpose of Compassionate Inquiry is to drill down to the core stories people tell themselves—to get them to see what story they are telling themselves unconsciously; what those beliefs are, where they came from; and guide them to

the possibility of letting go of those stories, or letting go of the hold those stories have on them...That's what Compassionate Inquiry is.[5]

During my ninety-hour CI practice, I had a practice partner. We would take turns and practice. The sequence included grounding work first to be present in the here and now and connect with our bodies.

One of the practice sessions would look like this: as a coach, I would ask my partner to set an intention for the session. It could be an area of our recent encounter or an incident she would like to explore, or an interaction she had with her child that she would be interested to inquire into. The illustrated incident brought up body sensation(s); she could describe how she felt (e.g., chest constriction, which might be matching with a suppressed emotion embedded in her body in the past). I would then invite her to check in and see if it was a familiar sensation. This led her to a childhood experience where her needs were unmet and her younger self made what happened back then about her. "I was not seen or heard back then. I experienced sadness; I made it mean I was not good enough..." As my partner experienced connection to herself, she was then slowly opening up to her vulnerability and emotions, and I could work with her on the healing from there.

---

5 Compassionate Inquiry, "The Approach." "Compassionate Inquiry®
   is a psychotherapeutic approach developed by Dr. Gabor Maté that
   reveals what lies beneath the appearance we present to the world."

"Compassionate Inquiry heals us, not just parents, when we feel safe in relationship, connected to our bodies, our breath, the present moment, and one another." This healing journey will lead us to "experience connection to ourselves and our children, as we open up to our vulnerability and emotions, and discover and express what is true for us."[6]

Ever since I have been on the path of the awakening journey, I have become more connected with my body. I find this approach effective because our *body does not lie*. Alice Miller, the author of *The Body Never Lies* explained, "The body is the guardian of the truth, our truth, because it carries the experience of a lifetime and ensures that we can live with the truth of our organism. With the aid of physical symptoms it forces us to engage cognitively with this truth so that we can communicate harmoniously with the child within, the child who lives on inside us..."[7]

The Compassionate Inquiry approach is not only an additional tool for me to do my own self-parenting and self-healing, but it also aids me in helping my clients to connect with their body when they may need a pause from verbal coaching.

Hypnotherapy

Hypnotherapy, or hypnosis, "is usually considered an aid to psychotherapy because the hypnotic state allows people to explore

---

6   Compassionate Inquiry, "The Approach."
7   Miller, *The Body Never Lies*, 31.

painful thoughts, feelings, and memories they might have hidden from their conscious minds."[8] I have also tapped into professional hypnotherapy sessions to work on inner wounds with repeated patterns, ones of which I have yet to identify the source. During the earlier years of my awakening journey, I was curiously interested in healing my inner child and past childhood wounds. How would I know it was my childhood wound? I could observe my "out of control" trigger because I could not explain where it came from (i.e., my blind spot). Once the emotional trigger was activated, I would get stuck for a while; it would keep coming back to disturb my peace. During my meditation session, I would feel some discomfort emotionally and physically. I could feel heaviness in my chest; at times, I would choose an alternative way to look inside my childhood wound, such as a professional hypnotherapy session.

During the session, my fellow Conscious Parenting coaching coursemate and certified hypnotherapist, Janet Philbin, would bring me to a safe place in my mind and guide me through

---

8   WebMD Editorial Contributors, "Mental Health and Hypnosis"; Clinical Practice Guideline for the Treatment of Posttraumatic Stress Disorder, "What is Psychotherapy?" I have included a further explanation of the psychotherapy in Chapter 2. According to the American Psychological Association, "Psychotherapy involves communication between patients and therapists that is intended to help people" find relief from emotional distress; seek solutions to problems such as family issues and career dissatisfaction; and modify ways of thinking and acting that are preventing them from working productively and enjoying personal relationships.

while narrowing down to a time and place when and where I got stuck, and help me heal from a particular childhood experience that kept me away from reaching my inner peace and authentic power. Every individual would have his or her own personalized hypnotherapy session and unique experience to explore and heal from.

As I heal layer after layer of my childhood wounds, I get reconnected with my true self, I reperceive life from wholeness and completeness, and my heart is filled with an abundance of love and gratitude.

Representational Systems for Raising Self-Consciousness Thinking

What are representational systems?

The concept of representational systems is one of the second major neurolinguistic programming (NLP) patterns discovered by Richard Bandler and John Grinder.[9] In business, Lindsey Agness translated it as *communication styles*.[10] According to O'Connor and Seymour,

> Representational systems are the basic building blocks of the NLP model. They are the processes by which human beings

---

9   Petrovici, "Effective Methods of Learning and Teaching."
    Neurolinguistic programming (NLP) claims that there is a connection between neurological processes (neuro), language (linguistic), and acquired behavioral patterns (programming), and that these can be changed to achieve specific goals in life.

10 Agness, *Change Your Business with NLP.*

perceive, represent or code and operate on the world. Seeing, hearing, feeling, smelling and tasting is how we experience the world around us and we recreate those same sensations in our mind, re-presenting the world to ourselves using our senses inwardly. Our representational systems encode, organize, store and attach meaning to perceptual input. Using our rep systems, we may either remember real past experiences or imagine possible (or impossible) future experiences.[11]

When I attended NLP practitioner's training in 2007, I realized that two of my dominant representational systems for my internal thinking process are auditory-digital based on self-talk, and kinesthetic. where I usually need to feel my way before taking action. Zooming into my discovery of self-talk, what I gleaned from this insight was that I could choose to turn off the noise in my head, especially those judgmental voices toward myself. For the first time in my life, I felt empowered to lower the volume of my endless negative self-talk.

To illustrate, here are some examples of predicate references that you might spot and identify yours or another person's representational system. If it is for yourself, knowing your representational system may help you in choosing your preferred language that matches your internal representational system and your thinking process when you are self-coaching/self-parenting. Or as you are able to identify another person's

---

11   O'Connor and Seymour, *Introducing NLP, 27.*

representational systems, you can make meaningful conversation because you are able to speak the same language, choosing words that match how the other party thinks internally while receiving the external information. The following is an extract from *NLP Made Easy: How to Use Neuro-Linguistic Programming to Change Your Life*:

Visual

Usually memorize by making pictures and less likely to be distracted by noise. Often have trouble remembering audible instructions. They are interested in how something looks and, even if they can remember the sound, they will most likely make a picture of it first. Examples of predicate references: See; Appear; Show.

Auditory

Typically are easily distracted by noise. They can repeat things back to you easily and learn just by listening. They like music and talking on the phone. Tone of voice and the words used are usually very important. You can upset them not by what you say but just by how you say it. Examples of predicate references: Hear; Resonate; Question.

Kinaesthetic

Often speak slowly and feel their way. They respond to physical rewards and touching. They memorize things best by doing it, walking through or rehearsing something. They will be interested in a solution that feels right or gives them a good gut feeling. Examples of predicate references: Feel; Grasp; Make contact.

Auditory-Digital

Tend to spend a fair amount of time talking to themselves. Superfluous information annoys them and they memorize by steps, procedures and sequences. They can also some-times exhibit characteristics of any other representational system. Examples of predicate references: Sense; Experience; Decide.[12]

We are receiving information through five senses: seeing, hearing, feeling, smelling, and tasting. As we gather information, we are making sense of our environment and the world we are living in. Our senses help us to make informed decisions about potential danger around our physical environment, or whether we are connecting with another party during a conversation, etc. We make internal pictures and thoughts represent the states. Let us pause and reflect on our own representational systems; we understand we "recreate those same sensations in our mind, re-presenting the world to ourselves using our senses inwardly."[13] We communicate to ourselves through creating our representational system, from the inputs received

---

12   Campbell, *NLP Made Easy*, 54–56.
13   Campbell, *NLP Made Easy*, 8.

from the external world via the sensory systems of what we see, hear, touch, smell, and feel.

Conscious Self-Parenting and Reflection

- Book a time with yourself, a loved one, or a close friend, and recall and share about a fond memory of yours. Get your loved one or close friend to help you spot any predicate references highlighted above from the book *NLP Made Easy*.
- If you share it with yourself, observe and notice these predicate references within your internal dialogue or in your journal, if you choose to pen it down.
- Which is/are your dominant representational system(s) (i.e., visual, auditory, kinesthetic, or auditory-digital)? There may be a primary one and a secondary one.

Having identified your dominant representational system(s), you may start and include the following mindful practices and meditation, integrate them into your daily routine, and practice over time. You will notice yourself becoming less judgmental and more sensitive while paying attention to sight, sound, smell, body sensations, feelings and thoughts, as well as the surrounding environment at the present moment, not overthinking about the past or future.

Conscious Self-Parenting and Reflection

- You may start by doing three minutes for each representational system (i.e., visual, auditory, kinesthetic, or auditory-digital). You are welcome to gradually increase your practice duration. This will help you strengthen your nonjudgmental "mental muscle."

- Observe your inner state. Are you easily getting distracted or paying more attention during each practice using a specific representational system? No right or wrong—if you are getting distracted, just accept those distractions and move on.

Visual—Nonjudgmental Seeing Practice

With your eyes comfortably open, turn your head and make a circular rotation anticlockwise, starting from the lower right corner to the top, then circle back to the lower right corner. Allow your eyes to peek at every corner without any judgment as you rotate your head. Receive everything that comes through your eyes without any judgment. (This is part of Wu Tao Dance Therapy's Sweet River movement meditation.)

Auditory—Nonjudgmental Listening Practice

Close your eyes and focus on your ears. First, turn your head and make a circular rotation clockwise of your head starting from the lower left corner to the top, then circle back to the lower left corner. Allow your ears to listen to every corner without any judgment as you rotate your head. Receive every sound that comes through your ears without any judgment. (This is part of Wu Tao Dance Therapy's Sweet River movement meditation.)

Kinesthetic—Walking Meditation

Walk in a straight line. Take one step at a time, slowly lift one of your feet up, and place it down while lifting the other foot up. Lift one foot up and place the other down interchangeably and slowly as you walk. Mind each step and focus on your feet; balance your pace. Receive every positive or negative feeling; feel the warmth or coolness of your feet without any judgment.

Auditory-Digital—Body Scan Meditation

Close your eyes. Let us do a body scan by focusing on your body sensation. Relax every muscle in your body, starting from the top of your head to your face, your jaw, your neck, your shoulder, your chest, your belly, your hip, your lap, your thighs, your knees, your shins, and down to your toes. Receive every sense and every thought in your *internal dialogue*:

- Q: Are the different parts of your body as you scan, such as facial muscles, relaxed?
- A: Feel different parts of your body as you scan, such as your facial muscles. Answer yes or no without any judgment.

Meditation

Meditation is a practice where an individual uses a technique—such as mindfulness or focusing the mind on a particular object, thought, or activity—to train attention and awareness, and achieve a mentally clear and emotionally calm and stable state.[14]

Meditation is a practice, and through this practice, one can develop different qualities, including mindfulness.[15]

Here are some of the meditation practices I have experienced, also listed in the table below (i.e., breathing meditation, walking meditation, and Vipassana meditation). Among all that I've mentioned, Vipassana or insight meditation has given me deep and insightful learning about myself. I began to learn about Vipassana meditation through my yearlong course, The Awakened Journey, with Dr. Shefali. I have since deepened my spiritual learning journey with Sola, a Chinese spiritual guide and practitioner.[16] I still practice these meditations interchangeably in my daily routine. What is Vipassana meditation? According to Sunnataram Forest Monastery,

---

14 Walsh and Shapiro, "Meeting of Meditative Disciplines."
15 Schultz, "5 Differences between Mindfulness and Meditation."
16 Sola lives in Toronto, Canada.

Vipassana means "seeing (passana) clear (vi)." The practice of Vipassana involves "observing" and "seeing." Where observing is the cause, seeing is the result. Sometimes we call "seeing" as the Realization of the Universal Truth; Change, Unstable and Not-Self. The result of realization is the Letting go of attachment which implies the Freedom/Liberation of the mind from Unhappiness (Nibbana/Nirvana). Every conditional thing in this world is subject to change, unstable and not under our direct control. These are called the Universal characteristics. People who don't realize these characteristics, and are not willing to accept change, will attach to things they love and try to resist change. Consequently they will suffer.

The practice of Vipassana is to gently allow the mind to "witness" the reality of body and mind in the most comfortable manner of Enlightenment. The mind will gradually accept the change, and the mind will realize the merit of letting go of attachment without feeling hurt. The final production is the Inner Peace (Nibbana).[17]

Here is a recent insight or inner wisdom I received from practicing Vipassana meditation when I was trying to clear my mind and to let go. I saw my egoic desire to search for the state of present-moment awareness, to interfere with the control of the acceptance of change and not-self or unself. In other words, I

17   Sunnataram Forest Monastery, "Mindfulness and Vipassana Meditation."

was holding on to achieve the outcome or final product, to keep the good feeling within me—the Inner Peace. The more I instructed my mind to let go, the more my mind was sucked into the attachment of the result of reaching the state of mind that "allows me to 'witness' the reality of body and mind in the most comfortable manner of Enlightenment." The desire in my mind was like a leech that would not let go. As I reflected, I was able to embrace what happened, the as-is, because I was aware of the cause of my attachment. What I can do differently next time is to wait patiently after I have sent a message in my mind to let go and to detach from my desired result—to reach inner peace.

What is enlightenment?

According to His Holiness the Dalai Lama, "Enlightenment is the awakening of the mind's true nature by the process of purifying thoughts, removing obscurations, and dispelling dissonant emotions."[18] Or small enlightenment like Thích Nhất Hạnh described during his interview with Oprah Winfrey, "Enlightenment is always there. Small enlightenment will bring great enlightenment. If you breathe in and are aware that you are alive—that you can touch the miracle of being alive—then that is a kind of enlightenment. Many people are alive but do not touch the miracle of being alive." To him, "enlightenment is the liberation from suffering that comes when you wake up to the true nature of reality."[19]

---

18   Kennedy, "Dalai Lama."
19   Winfrey, "Oprah Talks to Thích Nhất Hạnh."

As a conscious parent, I receive different aha moments or new learnings as I practice meditation. I am not saying that I will get enlightenment every time I practice meditation; however, when I do, it fills me with abundance and gratitude. Once, I was grateful about the love I have received from my daughter, Ally, since that magical touch during an early-hours feeding. At that moment, I felt warm in my heart and face, my heart was beating gently and steadily, and I was engrossed with this sensation and feeling loved at the moment. The next thought came in and reminded me about the love from Mother Nature: it was unconditional, it was selfless, or *not-self*; it was neutral without attaching to these good feelings. Having practiced meditation for about five years, I can gather a pattern of the effects of meditation as I integrate what I got from practicing into daily life. I observe this new pattern or new habit I can apply in planning my daily intention setting and routines. It is also useful for me to deal with every changing and demanding lifestyle when I get stuck, as I can gain insight(s) from meditation, i.e.:

Unself and clearing any judgmental thoughts →
Meditate in the morning or participate
in life in the present moment →
Wait for the inner wisdom to guide us →
Aha moment arises →
Journaling what we have learned.

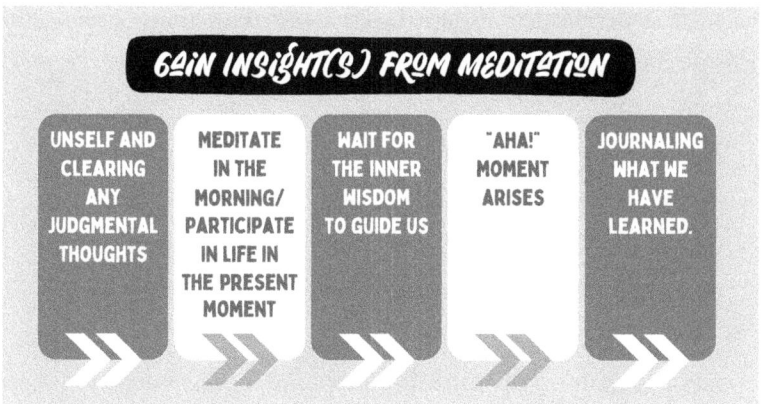

Separately, as I was journaling and reflecting on the new learning or enlightenment from meditation, I realized that I might have unconsciously become addicted to, if not began longing for, the love I received from my daughter. That good feeling I have been receiving, or I do not want to lose, may have unconsciously gotten me to want to be the "good" and "loving" mother, who at times just wants to be good and look good in front of my daughter. I am not saying that it is not good to have good feelings; however, if my intention is to hold on to good feelings in a selfish manner, or as an addiction, I may easily switch over to being a controlling mother and making sure my daughter loves me back to give me that good feeling. Subsequently, that Pleasing Jenny decides to cling to Ally to indulge herself with good feelings.

As I integrated meditation practice into my daily routine over the years, this is what made it possible for me to strengthen my mindfulness muscle. When I interact with my child, I am able to *shift in perspective*. Shapiro, Carlson, Astin, and Freedman term it as *reperceiving*.

> [R]eperceiving simply allows one to deeply experience each event of the mind and body without identifying with or clinging to it, allowing for "a deep, penetrative non-conceptual seeing into the nature of mind and world."[20]

As I check in on my mindfulness state, I can choose to let go of that clinging love and give my daughter space to be herself or do things she wants to do, rather than do things I want her to do because I am a good mother to her and she is supposed to "appreciate me" or "love me back."

Mindfulness

"Mindfulness is awareness that arises through paying attention, on purpose, in the present moment, and nonjudgmentally."[21] "Mindfulness (Chinese: 念) is the presence of heart," Jon Kabat-Zinn added.[22]

Yes, in the example I mentioned in the above section "Meditation," I shared my purpose and why I practice mindfulness. I aim to keep my inner peace while interacting with my daughter, and I do this by keeping open eyes, an open mind,

---

20 Kabat-Zinn, *Wherever You Go*; Shapiro et al., "Mechanisms of Mindfulness," 379.
21 Kabat-Zinn, *Wherever You Go*, 4.
22 Greater Good Science Center, "Jon Kabat-Zinn: What is Mindfulness?"

and an open heart. This shows I am paying attention in the moment, observing internal and external experiences—which allows me to set aside my own emotional baggage, judgments, and expectations of myself and my child.

To sum up, as one practices meditation over time, he or she can reach the calming state, be in the present moment, and be less judgmental toward themself and others. Shapiro, Carlson, Astin, and Freedman further stated in their study, "Mechanisms of Mindfulness," that the qualities we bring to the act of paying attention is crucial, "...persons can learn to attend to their own internal and external experiences, without evaluation or interpretation, and practice acceptance, kindness and openness even when what is occurring in the field of experience is contrary to deeply held wishes or expectations."[23]

When our state of awareness stays in the present moment, in a nonjudgmental way, we start to shift the way we see, think, and feel about the event, the conversation, or the person in front of us. We can stand back and simply witness what happened. With the shift of perspective (i.e., reperceiving) I become less controlled by particular emotions and thoughts that arise, and in turn am less likely to automatically follow them with habitual reactive patterns.[24] As a conscious parent, with mindfulness, I can observe my thoughts and internal self-talk; sometimes they are judgmental, sometimes they come from the place of

---

23 Shapiro et al., "Mechanisms of Mindfulness," 377.
24 Shapiro et al., "Mechanisms of Mindfulness."

love. From there, I am more responsive by making conscious decisions of my action or next step. With daily practice, we can strengthen our mindfulness muscles; subsequently, we can enhance our self-regulation and self-management skills that we can model for our children.

While parents are practicing mindfulness, it motivates children to practice mindfulness as they watch us at the side. As I enjoy connecting with nature, appreciating beauty and simple happiness in life, I tend to speak aloud about my thoughts and my point of views in front of Ally. Gradually, she learns to appreciate beauty and other values from our day-to-day interaction. For example, one time Ally and I were eating tomatoes. She was appreciating how juicy the tomatoes were, and making this satisfying expression, "Life is so good." I could see her joy in tasting the tomatoes; both of her eyebrows and the corners of the mouth were raised up high. Happiness can be very simple; it usually comes from simple experiences that give you joy and wonder and make you appreciate being alive. Can you see the benefits of mindfulness practice for our everyday interaction with our children?

Psychotherapy

According to Dr. Bernard Golden, psychotherapy and mindfulness meditation are different, while they may have similar goals and practices:

Psychotherapy looks at the larger picture of our self and "script" by which we live. Mindfulness and mindfulness

meditation help us to become more aware of the inner work-
ings of our minds—enhancing our capacity to recognize,
observe and experience our thoughts, feelings and sensations without our being overwhelmed by them. At the same
time, it can help us train our brain to make us less reactive
to what we observe, thus allowing us to more assertively
choose how we wish to define our lives. Are we genuinely
open, curious and non-judgmental? It often takes great
self-reflection and personal work that might include psychotherapy to free us up to be more fully present in our lives in
general—including when we sit on the cushion.[25]

Psychotherapy is a talk or verbal therapy. "It begins with
some discussion of a person's background and the concerns
that led him or her to seek help."[26] Areas of help include finding
relief from emotional distress, seeking solutions to problems
such as family issues or career dissatisfaction, and modifying
ways of thinking and acting that are preventing them from
working productively and enjoying personal relationships.
There are many different kinds of therapy with similar goals
in helping people feel better and think constructively, such as
making a choice with clarity and being more aware of the potential consequence(s), or taking a different action and gaining a

---

25 Golden, "Mindfulness Meditation and Psychotherapy."
26 Clinical Practice Guideline for the Treatment of Posttraumatic Stress
    Disorder, "What is Psychotherapy?"

sense of competence to solve problems in life. At times, therapy helps people to have the courage to take a new action or adjust their attitude by replacing new scripts such as to be the author of their life, rather than powerlessly to allow themselves to be victims in situations or life events.

Here are some of the different types of therapy I have experienced and practiced:

Dance/Movement Therapy

According to Karkou et al., "Unlike verbal psychotherapy, and unlike the most prevalent forms of psychotherapy recommended for depression such as cognitive behavioral therapy, Dance Movement Therapy (DMT) does not require considerable cognitive and linguistic skills from the client. Therefore, it can potentially bypass social or cultural barriers. DMT may offer a way to work through issues that are difficult to articulate or are buried in the unconscious because they are painful, frightening, or simply difficult to access and address through cognitive means."[27]

Additionally, the American Dance Therapy Association further detailed what dance therapy is:

Dance is an art form that has been around since the beginning of time, its purpose has been used for healing and spiritual rituals and progressed to entertainment for others. As

---

27 Karkou et al., "Effectiveness of Dance Movement Therapy."

time has passed, dance has been brought back as a healing method, specifically a type of therapy, to help those in need today. Dance movement therapy (DMT) is defined as the psychotherapeutic use of movement to promote emotional, social, cognitive, and physical integration of the individual, for the purpose of improving health and well-being.

Furthermore,

Movement is a language, our first language. Nonverbal and movement communication begins in utero and continues throughout the lifespan. Dance/movement therapists believe that nonverbal language is as important as verbal language and use both forms of communication in the therapeutic process.[28]

I experienced it myself; I can calm my inner weather better when I move my body. These movements can be walking, structured or unstructured dance, or engaging in obstacle course exercises.

Wu Tao Dance Therapy

Wu Tao Dance Therapy is the first dance therapy I experienced and practiced that helped me connect with the flow of my

---

28 American Dance Therapy Association, "What is Dance/Movement Therapy?"

inner energy and body sensations. There was a natural flow of abundance and relaxation after practicing it. Wu Tao Dance Therapy was founded by Michelle Locke in 2001. She integrated dance, shiatsu, and oriental medicine to help people heal and restore balance.

Each one-hour session consists of:

1. Warm-up through "hara mindful breathing"
2. Element dance movement that promotes the circulation of the meridian system
3. Guided meditation and/or art therapy

The meridian system is a concept in traditional Chinese medicine (TCM); they are paths through which the life-energy known as "qi" (ch'i) flows.

I received a certification as a Wu Tao Dance Therapy instructor in 2019. I was attracted to it mainly for three reasons:

1. Self-expression
2. Alternative means to connect with my body
3. Self-care to enhance physical and mental well-being

In fact, ever since I practiced it and provided lessons to others, the feedback has again and again been that dancing Wu Tao allows people to feel connected on a deeper level, and we receive the oneness with a greater sense of mind-body-soul connection. At the end of each session, everyone is getting what they may need for that present moment: for some, relaxation; some may be easing their tensed muscles; some may be releasing troubled emotions; and some may be receiving courage or a new discovery or direction upon their inaction, etc. A few may start from numbness, not feeling anything as they listen to others, and wonder why they do not receive anything. However, when practicing over time, they slowly open up, and the next thing is waiting for them to muster the courage to share what they observe or receive via their mind, body, emotion, feeling and/or energy.

How does Wu Tao Dance Therapy connect with parenting? During one of the online dance sessions, one of my clients was practicing water dance. Many movements flowed smoothly, and she was following well with the group and the music. During the debrief, our conversation went like this:

Mother/Client: I do not think I follow and dance well. I am unable to show the gentle flow of water movement. I just cannot.

Me: Can you share with me more about the gentle flow of water movement?

Mother/Client: I am supposed to dance as gently as water.

Me: I would like to invite you to think about other forms of water. For example, a waterfall, white water, or rough water. Water can be ice, too.

Mother/Client: Hmm...I did not think of it that way.

Me: Let us connect this preexisting belief with your

parenting. Have you ever felt like my child "should be x," so when your child is not listening to you, or matching your shoulds or expectations, you feel discouraged as a mother? However, you overlook that your child is his own being; he has the freedom to change or to be in different states. Just like how you have an expectation of yourself to dance gently like water. However, you overlook that water may be in other forms and states.

Mother/Client (in deep thought): Yes, yes.

Art Therapy

From Holly Tiret's article "The Benefits Art Therapy Can Have on Mental and Physical Health":

The therapeutic potential of art is vast and applicable to individuals of all age groups. Art therapy, formally established since the 1940s, serves as a means for clients to delve into their inner thoughts, feelings and experiences through creative expression.

A literature review on art therapy, published in Cureus, reveals that therapists frequently assign patients' freeform art expressions to help with discussions about the images and encourage introspection. When combined with talk therapy, art therapy aids individuals in managing intense emotions, fostering self-awareness and self-worth, and decreasing stress and anxiety. This therapeutic approach encompasses a wide range of creative expressions, such as dance, music, drawing, painting, coloring, sculpting and more.[29]

Wu Tao Dance Therapy instructors use art therapy interchangeably with meditation during a Wu Tao Dance session. Through art therapy, participants are encouraged to express their inner dialogues, energy felt after a dance session, or anything that comes to their mind at the present moment using simple drawing with a single color or colored pencils or markers. All the creative expressions each participant recorded for themselves are uniquely presented. At times, these drawings help the participant to see some "answer" they were looking for at that juncture of decision-making. Other times, as the audience listens to others sharing, one may also get an answer, or discover some new learning, through their "selective" listening and seeing that suits their present state of awareness.

There were times I drew a tree with roots at the end of Wu Tao Dance Therapy; it reflected my inner steadiness and inner strength. The visual image reflected my inner world. Indeed, with the state of mind, as I observed myself interacting with my daughter, I had a sense of clarity and firmness. I could see the space I gave to Ally honoring her sovereignty and not interrupting her natural flow. Subsequently, that expansive feeling and energy flow activated my warmth, and it was ready to give to anyone around me.

---

29 Tiret, "The Benefits Art Therapy Can Have on Mental and Physical Health."

Journaling

According to the Center for Journal Therapy, journaling is "the purposeful and intentional use of reflective writing to further mental, physical, emotional, and spiritual health and wellness."[30]

Self-coaching or self-parenting sections designed and integrated throughout this book are a form of self-directed journal therapy with guided questions; they help to facilitate internal dialogues. It may be different from you keeping a journal, and yet, the intention of questions is designed to provide an exercise to do your own purposeful and intentional self-reflective writing. It may also be a therapeutic journaling process that helps you write down your thoughts and feelings about your personal experiences and observations. This healing process through writing does not rely on the words penned, but on the words in the mind of the person who utilizes journal therapy.

Another example of recommended activities for journal therapy is Dr. Robert Emmons's gratitude journal and expression.

According to Dr. Robert Emmons, with his more than ten years worth of research on gratitude, it has shown him that,

> When life is going well, gratitude allows us to celebrate and magnify the goodness. But what about when life goes badly? In the midst of the economic maelstrom that has gripped our country, I have often been asked if people can—or even should—feel grateful under such dire circumstances.

30 GoodTherapy, "Journal Therapy."

My response is that not only will a grateful attitude help—it is essential. In fact, it is precisely under crisis conditions when we have the most to gain by a grateful perspective on life.

In the face of demoralization, gratitude has the power to energize.

In the face of brokenness, gratitude has the power to heal.

In the face of despair, gratitude has the power to bring hope.

In other words, gratitude can help us cope with hard times.[31]

More often than usual, journaling is a way of integration for me. For example, as I have gotten some glimpse of new self-discovery or insights during meditation, dance, or therapy, I would journal about the insights and connect back to my current interpretation of my life, myself, or my roles as mother, coach, daughter, wife, woman, etc. These inner conversations allow me to modify (e.g., clear or let go), embrace, enhance or reset, and integrate my perspective, my mind (i.e., the flow of information and energy), my attitude (i.e., thinking, feeling, and being), or my values-based action.

I hope by now you have gotten an idea of a variety of possible healing techniques, methods, and practices available. Here's an overview of the effective healing methods I have experienced (there are other methods such as music therapy, play therapy, somatic therapy, and more to be explored).

---

31   Emmons, "How Gratitude Can Help."

	Meditation*	Mindfulness	Therapy
What This Is	Meditation is a practice.	Mindfulness is a quality; it helps you tune into your surroundings and increase your present-moment awareness.	• Psychotherapy is a talk or verbal therapy • Art therapy and dance/movement therapy are types of creative or nonverbal psychotherapy; they can be combined with talk/verbal therapy • Journal therapy is purposeful and intentional use of reflective writing
How to Practice	• Body scan meditation • Breathing meditation • Vipassana meditation • Movement meditation such as walking meditation	Everyday activities such as drinking, eating, walking, talking, standing, sitting, washing dishes, taking showers, cooking, etc.	• Find a therapist who connects with you well, and who's methods suit you • Wu Tao Dance Therapy with meditation and art therapy • Journal therapy such as gratitude journal
Why Care and Practice	• Gain better concentration and stress management skills • Change different aspects of attention and mindfulness	• Gain better stress management skills • Decrease emotional reactivity • Improve focus; increase working memory • Build better relationships	Psychotherapy: • Find relief from emotional distress. • Seek solutions to problems such as family issues and career dissatisfaction • Modify ways of thinking and acting that are preventing you from working productively and enjoying personal relationships

Why Care and Practice (continued)	• Increase self-awareness • Improve emotional well-being	Gain relaxation and concentration of the mind in sitting meditation much more easily.	Dance/Movement Therapy:[†] • Self-awareness: be more aware and sensitive to your surroundings and build stronger inner connections with yourself • Social integration: enables you to relate with your environment and make connections with people around you Art Therapy, combined with Talk Therapy, can help people:[**] • Deal with strong emotions • Increase self-awareness and self-worth • Decrease stress and anxiety Journal Therapy:[††] • Increase awareness and insight • Promote change and growth • Further develop one's sense of self
When and Where to Practice	Your designated time and place	Anytime, anywhere	The agreed time and place with your therapists or coaches. At other times, you could do self-coaching.

* Cherry, "How Meditation Impacts Your Mind and Body."
† American Dance Therapy Association, "What is Dance/Movement Therapy?"
** Tiret, "Benefits Art Therapy Can Have."
†† GoodTherapy, "Journal Therapy."

Furthermore, some of them can be mixed and matched to suit your needs and preference. Here are some mixed and matched examples; one was mentioned earlier such as Wu Tao Dance Therapy combining dance/movement therapy with art therapy, where healing is processed through nonverbal communication and creative expressions.

Another example is combining meditation and journaling; further elaboration is given next.

Combining Meditation and Journaling

The following practices can be set as part of your daily routine combining breathing, meditation, and journaling to get in touch with your inner voices. Or, use them to sink in with your heart and body by quieting down your mind and detaching from your own judging mind, and kickstarting your inner connection.

Conscious Self-Parenting and Reflection

Set aside five minutes for a breathing meditation daily. You can schedule it in the morning after you wake up, and/or before bedtime. You can also consider adding five minutes incrementally until a duration that you feel comfortable  sitting with yourself; in fact, it may bring you joy even thinking about spending this time with yourself. When you start feeling stressful about spending time with yourself through breathing meditation, you may consider reducing and adjusting the duration. Please be kind and gentle with yourself, even if you miss or skip some days; just resume the practice the next day. When you are at the start of the practice, do give yourself a pat on your shoulder and tell yourself, "Well begun is half done."

Let us get started:

- Adjust your sitting posture. You may sit on a chair and place your feet flat on the floor, with feet and knees roughly hip width apart. Or if you choose to sit on the floor, you may sit on a cushion where you place your hips a bit higher than the thighs and knees, and cross your legs.
- Sit up straight, so that your head and neck are in line with your spine.
- Place both of your arms shoulder width apart, and relax your shoulders.
- You may choose to open or close your eyes.
- Use your breaths to bridge the inner and outer spaces until you are one with those spaces. And observe your breaths as described under "Breathing Technique" to follow.
- Tell yourself you fully and unconditionally accept yourself. You can also say this to yourself silently. Choose phrases that resonate with you most. For example: *I am whole. I am complete. I am enough. I am loved. I am worthy, because I am. I am home.*
- How does your body feel? Is there any body sensation? Hold this compassion within you.
- If you would like, you can journal about your thoughts, your feelings, and your body sensation(s) as per what you have observed.

Breathing Technique

Observe your breaths:

- Focus on your in and out breaths as they pass your philtrum (the midline between your upper lip and nose), or
- Focus on the wavelike sensation of your chest rising and falling with your breath.

This list is not all-encompassing. There are many other activities/practices that would also allow you to create space for you to get comfortable with your uncomfortable feeling(s). Take some time to play and see what feels right for you and to heal your inner child.

By increasing your awareness in your daily practice, you will soon build up your emotional regulation muscles that help you detach from your negative thoughts. Just like me, you can make a conscious choice to stop communicating (with yourself or others) when you catch yourself engaging in negative thoughts. You can choose to respect your own emotional boundaries and communicate nonjudgmentally with your inner child, your real children, or people around you. The positive energy will start flowing in and out of your body; the first ripple of positive change starts within you.

three

FROM PAIN*FULL* TO PAIN*LESS*

"What is pain?"[1]

What would be your first response to this question? Many of us may think of physical pain, such as headaches. The next thing we may think about is finding ways to relieve headaches, such as taking painkillers or applying

---

1   "The words *pain* and *suffering* are often used interchangeably. For example, definitions of pain in the dictionary include bodily suffering, mental/emotional suffering, or distress, and suffering is defined as the bearing of pain or distress. It is understandable that these words are intertwined in relation to cancer patients in pain. However, there are distinctions. Pain is a physical sensation or signal indicating an event within the body. Suffering is the interpretation of that event and...

various ointments. In short, we want to get rid of pain. How about heartaches/emotional pain? What do you do to relieve your heartaches? No painkiller or ointment would relieve you from heartache. Some may find ways to cope with or numb their heartaches, such as binge drinking, binge-watching TV, or indulging themselves with endless tubs of ice cream. Yes, indulging ourselves with food that would never satisfy us or make us feel full. We call it "emotional hunger"; it relies on food to soothe the pain. "Common signs of emotional hunger: (1) felt more in your head; (2) strong and specific cravings; (3) comes on quickly and feels urgent; (4) may happen even if you just ate; (5) not always satisfied by eating."[2] Some extreme cases involve taking drugs or dealing with pain by physically hurting themselves.

Having embarked on this personal development and awakening journey as a conscious parent, the experience has been both a painful and joyful journey for me. To let go of who I am not, who I think my father would want me to be, who I had been trying to become "my entire life" was painful, especially because I was holding onto this for so long and living it like it was my reality. To accept who I am and remove the judgment about myself was hard and painful. I have since become a courageous warrior to face my pains, to find ways to heal myself, and have relieved my pain bit by bit. Every "shedded skin" is a

...involves thoughts, beliefs, or judgments, and reflects the human experience of pain. Pain can cause suffering when it is uncontrolled or persists," Siler et al., "Pain and Suffering."
2   University of New Mexico, "Food for Thought."

way to get closer to myself; every healing process is a release of the past painful experiences. It was the first time I showed up courageously for myself after my awakened journey, facing any pain that may be retriggered along the way. I posted the following to the "Year of Awakened Heart" course closed group; it was the first step in ensuring my voice was heard:

7 July 2017

Good morning, tribe!

Today, I am stepping into my discomfort zone for the very first time to express my gratitude and appreciation to our awakened heart community.

Thank you, Dr. Shefali, for your deep commitment to creating "The Year of Awakened Heart" course. Through your teaching, I now see a totally different level of freedom in my soul. I am humbled by this profound experience.

Thank you, Suzi, for your words in one of the meditation sessions: "I am enough; I am worth it; I am home—because I am."[3] These words brought me back to the present moment.

Thank you, tribe members, for sharing your discoveries and experiences with me. They've touched, moved, and inspired me.

---

3   Suzi Lula, spiritual therapist, author of *The Motherhood Evolution.* She was a cofacilitator of Dr. Shefali's mediation sessions.

Thank you, Francesca, for the "Guided Inner Child Visualization." This visualization exercise got me to see, hear, and touch my inner child clearly. For years, I felt so alone. I realized I was an emotionally sensitive child, and my needs were not met. I was not acknowledged, recognized, or seen. I felt (emotionally) abandoned or betrayed. One of my childhood decisions was to "lock" myself up in a "safe place" (my comfort zone) internally, so that there was no hope, no pain, no harm, etc. That is why I felt uncomfortable in front of others, I got super nervous and avoided self-disclosure to the outside world. That day as I did the visualization, my adult self said to my inner child, "It is okay, everything is going to be all right. I will hold your hand, walk this life together with you without letting go. It is okay, I am here." My adult self opened my (inner child's) heart up with a sense of security and *eased my fear.*

"My inner child, you can step out from the 'dungeon' now; come fly with me, *experience the sky and the world with me,*" said my adult self lovingly.

All this while, my inner child might have been waiting for someone to show up and set me free; however, there were no signs at all that any "heroes" would come to rescue me. Not until my daughter touched my face during one of the feeding times when she was a few months old. I was over-whelmed by her "magical touch"; I felt her unconditional love and realized unconditional love was bidirectional, parent to child and child to parent. My girl (she is now seven

years old) loves me with all her heart and accepts me unconditionally for who I am.

Of course, not until here at awakened hearts, through Dr.
Shefali and the tribe here, did I get to see my inner child and
heal and love her with all my heart.

May all of us continue to embrace this discomfort zone,
raise and face our inner child courageously, and uncover our
truths. Love you, tribe!

THE STRENGTH IN PAIN

"Do you see me?"

"Do you hear me?"

"Can you see how hard I work for your approval, Dad?"

These inner voices stayed with me from childhood well into
my thirties, before I became a mother. I did not consciously
know that I had been trying to prove myself and my worth to
my dad by getting one better-paying job after another. I just had
this undercurrent of belief that said everything I did could be
improved and should be better.

In 2014, due to self-acceptance and connection with my true
self through Conscious Parenting coaching and meditations, I
finally realized that there was no end to this chase. I was not
looking for good incomes to improve my quality of life. I was
hoping my dad would say, "Jenny, you have done well. I am so
proud of you." But that day never came. Most importantly, I
no longer need that day to come, as I have the courage to face

my truth—accept who I am and who I am not, and no longer pursue becoming someone whom I think others want me to be.

I did not yet realize that I could choose to love others the way I wanted to be loved, the way I was loving my daughter. My love for her goes beyond providing for her basic needs as a mother. Loving her means I am willing to face my ugly truth about the "fake me" I project, my false self. I am willing to tear that inner me apart until the *real* me, my true self, is revealed once more. Because of my love for my daughter, I am ready to face my pain, boiled down to common fears: making mistakes, not being loved, being misunderstood, and not being good enough. I was also afraid that others might find out I was not kind, and that I might be a selfish being who was presumptuously seeking social approval. My inner judgment was loud, and I suppressed my "greed" and tried hard to be a "good girl."

Because I love my daughter, I am working on cleaning up my mess and letting go of these fears.

At this moment, let us take a pause and give you some time to reflect.

Conscious Self-Parenting and Reflection

- When was the last time you booked and spent time with yourself? How was it for you? Were you comfortable being with yourself?
- Make and spend time with yourself

regularly; hear your inner dialogue about yourself. Make a list and describe each version (e.g., Timid Jenny Jan. 2022).
- Describe something you like or dislike about yourself. What are some of these likable/unlikable qualities? Why did you like or dislike those versions of you?
- Draw connections between your fears and versions of yourself. Are these fears linked with different versions of you? Are there things you are hiding or afraid of others finding out?

THE ROOT OF MY FEARS AND HOW
YOU CAN RECOGNIZE YOURS

I know why I was so afraid of making mistakes back then.

When I was eight years old, my sisters and I stayed at my uncle's house and spent time with my cousins when my parents were busy. When I played the Old Maid card game with my cousins, they would laugh and tease me when I picked the Old Maid card as the last person.

"Why do you not know such a simple thing?! Hahaha..."

"You are an old maid! You are an old maid! You would not be able to get married as you are an old maid! Hahaha..."

Of course, they were just having fun and did not mean to hurt me. Still, getting the wrong answer filled me with dread as if something serious were going to happen to me. From then on, making a mistake or giving a wrong answer made me feel just like fearing picking an Old Maid card, which could lead to being teased and laughed at like a silly old maid. I decided that I would never make another stupid mistake. I studied hard and avoided saying anything that made me feel or look stupid.

Those pains followed me into my adult life. I cared so much about what others thought of me. During work meetings, I only said what I thought people wanted to hear. I made sure what I said was supported by evidence, using only credible sources. I pushed myself hard in my twenties and early thirties and performed well. By age thirty-four, I felt burnt out. I wanted to do more than please others; I wanted to please myself. I started looking for meaning in life. I went deeper, asking, *Who am I? Why am I here? That was about the same time I decided to conceive a child and become a mother after seven years of marriage.*

After becoming a mother and receiving unconditional love from my child, I have received more clarity of my purpose and meaning in life. I hope Ally can grow up with fewer childhood wounds. If anyone could not understand my choices after my awakening, here is what I told myself. It has become my "energizer" when I am down:

I will keep a candle lit in my heart, even when there is wind, even when other people want to blow my light out. I will protect this light in me and help light others. Together, we will light up the darkness and the "treasure" inside. We will not wait until the next lifetime to connect.

I hold insight in my heart about life, consciousness, my purpose, unity, hope, simplicity, love, and my inner child. I have a clear vision to unleash my true self.

Conscious Self-Parenting and Reflection

What was your greatest pain in life? Have you overcome and/or embraced it? If so, what did you do? If not, is it okay to accept the pain as-is? Below, you'll find a list of things you can do while you are feeling and facing the pain:

- Just sit with yourself, own your emotions, and cry it all out
- Meditate
- Go for a hike/walk in nature
- Talk to someone about it
- Help others
- Draw
- Dance along with your favorite music
- Journal
- Exercise
- Try a self-compassion exercise (see the "Tools & Resources" section)
- Listen to your body if it is "telling" you to go for a walk, take a rest, exercise, etc.
- Take a nice warm bath/shower
- Write a gratitude list and focus on what you already have. Start with "I am grateful for…"

- Revisit your vision board that captured your life goals
- Watch videos of wisdom teachers (see a list of wisdom teachers at the back of the book)
- Look for Conscious Parenting coaches to get clarity on old patterns that keep you from growing and how to be in the present moment.

Do you have an "energizer" or a coping strategy that helps you to pick yourself up when you are feeling down? If not, take the time to construct one now.

More than usual, you may not be aware of where all these pains come from. To be more aware of them, you can start observing your triggers and when you become emotionally drained or intensified unknowingly. Start knowing your pains, observe how you have been habitually going back to the same patterns to help you "get rid of" pain. To pay attention to the opportunity to heal yourself, get closer to your true self along this self-discovery journey. There is a fine line between getting rid of your pain and healing your pain. Can you differentiate these two? To get rid of emotional pain, people might be trying to avoid pain by numbing themselves through addictions such as binge shopping, binge-watching TV, binge drinking, taking drugs, etc. Or to the other end, people might be cutting themselves because the issues are emotionally too painful to bear. They are unable to stay in the present moment and are unconsciously led by pain, as it brings them back to the past—the past where their wound was first created, where they were emotionally hurt because something happened from outside that led to something happening inside of them. "Addictions always originate in pain, so the question is never really why the addiction, but why the pain," said Dr. Gabor Maté.[4] Why the pain? It could be due to an individual's perceived reality or interpretation that they were not loved, they were not worthy, they were not important. In addiction, people might be hoping that things will turn out differently. They might also regard themselves as victims of what happened.

As for healing, people are gradually facing the pain; they may first try to regulate their pain on their own using the "energizer" mentioned earlier. However, they are also resourceful to seek professional help to heal the pain; they are trying to break the habitual patterns that bring them back to their pain again and again. They are ready to take the power back to heal their wounds from inside out; they are heroes and heroines, the true selves, who are transformed from pain through a healing journey. Collecting personalities can be one of your first awareness clues in identifying your habitual patterns of avoiding pain like a victim. On the other hand, you may also be able to collect heroes and heroines who give you inner strength to shed the layers of your egoic or false selves—these false selves who have a purpose to keep you small, "protect" you, and create self-helplessness in you.

---

4   Curry, "My Mother's Addiction."

WHERE DOES PAIN BRING US?

Along my awakened and Conscious Parenting journey, I get to know my pain more. Through wisdom teachings and mindful practices, I get to connect with my inner being.

Here is my healing process:

- **How Pain Formed.** Many pains formed in my past; they were connected with my wounded inner child, as my needs were not met as a child. Something happened to me in the external environment (e.g., my parents did or did not do or say things); as a result, I interpreted my unmet needs as my parents did not love me, I was not worthy, or I was not important. What happened inside of me formed a perception of how I saw myself and constructed a limiting belief about me.

- **Feeling and Dealing with Pain.** Along my growing up journey, another event happened; it uncovered the pain within me, which connected with my limiting belief about myself (e.g., "I am not worthy or good enough"). Instead of staying in the present moment of observing and understanding what happened, my wounded inner child with pain was triggered, and it brought me back to my past and stood in between my adult self and present moment.

- **Healing or Resisting/Avoiding Pain.** As I am on the path of my healing journey, I can activate my mindfulness (this muscle has been strengthened through my daily practice of meditation) and reconnect with myself; it brings me back to the present moment, so that I can make a conscious decision on my next step.

You may ask as you are still in the midst of understanding your wounded inner child, your pain, and the source of pain, what do you do? You can start paying attention and building your awareness of your present habitual patterns in dealing with pain. Consider you may have been trying to avoid your pain by numbing through online gaming, binge shopping, binge drinking, or drug addiction, or distracting yourself from life through binge-watching or self-harm as a way of stopping emotional pain. If you are getting stuck at the same place again and again, even though you told yourself loud and clear that, "This will be my last episode, last glass of wine, last game, last shopping item," etc., please pause and ask yourself a different question. Or, make a compassionate inquiry: *Where does this painful feeling come from?* or *What am I running away from again and again that I have to rely on this addiction to cover up for me?* When you start inserting a pause or asking a different question, there comes an opportunity for you to recover yourself through choosing healing.

In the healing process, because you know and feel there is a tiny crack of light shining through the cloudy dark gloomy sky, it gives you hope and inner knowing that this will soon be over. Furthermore, in hope, you get to see your strengths that your childhood wounds bring you. It takes much commitment, hard work, and courage to heal. As much as we can as parents, do not pass on suffering to your children.

A study published in the *Journal of Child Psychology and Psychiatry* concluded that:

> Caregiver internalising and PTSD symptoms are important mechanisms through which caregiver trauma and hardship affect parenting behaviours. Emotion dysregulation is a shared mechanism linking caregivers' mental health problems with parenting behaviours that reflect acceptance and rejection of the child. Emotion regulation is indicated as a key target for prevention of adverse effects of caregiver trauma on mental health and child wellbeing.[5]

Another study also concluded that unresolved trauma in mothers has intergenerational effects:

> A significant proportion of clinical work revolves around helping patients in the resolution of childhood trauma. Our study reaffirms that unresolved trauma is associated with insecure attachment in both mothers and their offspring, while providing the first preliminary evidence that attachment reorganization may lessen the risk of insecure attachment in the offspring.[6]

5   Jensen et al., "Intergenerational Impacts of Trauma," 989.
6   Iyengar et al., "Unresolved Trauma in Mothers."

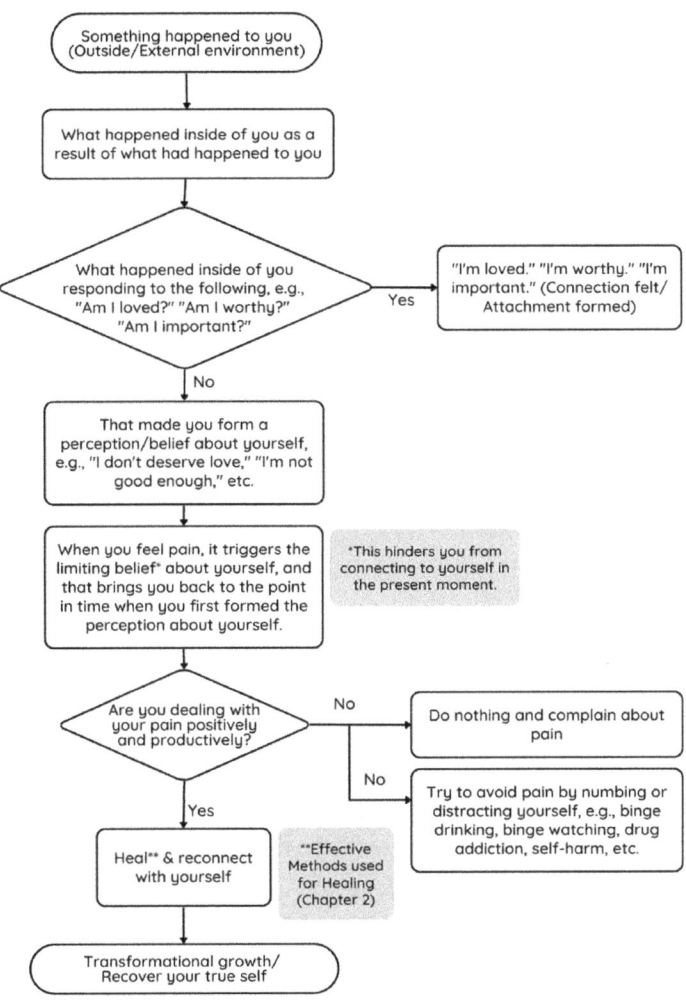

Where does pain bring us?

ALBUM OF DIFFERENT PERSONALITIES EXERCISE

Have you ever noticed that day in and day out, you are carrying different personalities in you to help you get things done or receive love and acceptance in your deepest desires? From your triggers collection, you get to know yourself more through identifying and labeling your different personalities. These personalities usually help you deal with your pain. You can label each of your personalities for easy recall purposes and share:

1. When and where do you see this personality appear: observe the event, what situation, with whom, or at a specific setting or environment.

2. What does it do for you: does it help you fight, avoid, or numb your pain? For instance, to avoid pain from feeling *You are not enough. You are not worthy.* One of your personalities might try to keep you small and "safe" in your comfort zone. Alternatively, you might also have a personality trying to prove to others that *You are worthy*, so you might set up a big goal and seem to "work hard" every day. However, day after day, you did not get closer to accomplishing your goal.

3. Are you getting along well or not? Are you resisting a specific personality? Why? Or, are you actually feeling the power and positivity when this personality appears?

4. What do you want to do about it at this juncture? You can decide to have the personality stay in your collection, to accept it and thank it, to put it aside, to keep in view, etc.

Here are some examples of how the above personalities showed up in my life:

At work, I needed to make a cold call to a new childcare center on a certain day to introduce my services. I procrastinated! *Dreamy Jenny* sneaked into my mind unconsciously and whispered into my ears, "You have bigger things you want to achieve in life. It is okay to delay a little and do it tomorrow." Once that happened, I got distracted and went on to do other things. I did not even do my perceived "bigger thing," such as developing a new parenting program, that could possibly have made a bigger impact on the parents. Later, because I kept telling myself I needed more time to sort out the "bigger thing," I kept giving myself excuses and pushing it off. It became a vicious cycle, and I was constantly in the rat race of not having enough time to do the "bigger thing" or things that are important to me. I could see where my pain came from, as I could not fulfill and honor my word to do the bigger thing; I would reprimand myself using my judgmental and critical voices. Soon after, my *Disconnected Jenny* would stay a few days before I would become *Calm Jenny*, who comes from a place of love and who wants to do bigger things in life. With shorter time spent in victim mode and clarity of what gets us stuck, we can get out of our vicious cycle in a shorter time frame and be more compassionate toward ourselves for going off track. We can then be *painless*.

PERSONALITIES ALBUM

CALM JENNY

1 When and where do you see this personality?

When I am having anxiety

2 What does it do for you? (hide/seek/show up/etc.)

Calm me down with love and compassion, and say, "Do not worry; I got this."

3 Are you and this personality getting along well or not?

Yes, I love Calm Jenny!

Calm Jenny helps me to support my daughter and show up in front of her with compassion and deep commitment. Prior to this, I received true and unconditional compassion from Calm Jenny to overcome some of my emotional pains.

I noticed there are two versions of Calm Jenny when she shows up:

 When Calm Jenny comes from a place of love and true self, she is compassionate and shares unconditional love.

 When Calm Jenny comes from a place of fear, she puts on a mask to show calmness on the outside and to show others she has everything in control. Deep inside, she is anxious and judgmental about things that happened to her.

4 What do you want to do about it at this juncture?

Stay

SELF-COMPASSIONATE JENNY

1 When and where do you see this personality?

When I feel abundant and self-loved.

2 What does it do for you? (hide/seek/show up/etc.)

I can notice my physiological reaction; I feel constricted in my chest area. Emotionally, I may be feeling upset, angry, or frustrated when I have an expectation of how things should be, and things have not gone well.

3 Are you and this personality getting along well or not?

I have learned to hold the space for these emotions, or to create time and space to do Wu Tao's Wood Element dance, and allow my emotion and unwanted energy to release through dance movement.

4 What do you want to do about it at this juncture?

Stay

---

1 When and where do you see this personality?

When I need to deal with "reality" such as financial reporting, administrative work, cold calling, etc.

2 What does it do for you? (hide/seek/show up/etc.)

On the surface, Dreamy Jenny tells me to avoid "trivial things" that relate to sales and business development, and money matters. Dreamy Jenny usually says, "I have more 'meaningful things' to do." Deep down I was fearful to find out that I might not be worthy of success. I could then "blame" my lack of success on the endless trivial things that I had to attend to, instead of taking action to achieve the mission or business goal I set for myself.

DREAMY JENNY

3 Are you and this personality getting along well or not?

This is an unhealthy relationship between my mission and business. In the long run, it would delay my action to bring my services to the community. Or worse, Dreamy Jenny would just stay in my head, and I would never clear action items on my to-do list or execute my action plan.

4 What do you want to do about it at this juncture?

I will say "hi" to Dreamy Jenny and put her aside when she shows up.

1 When and where do you see this personality?

When I want to avoid facing the negativity in me. Or I am afraid of confrontation of my weakness.

DISCONNECTED JENNY

2 What does it do for you? (hide/seek/show up/etc.)

Disconnected Jenny wants me to to hide and be an inner child runaway when facing my vulnerabilities, my loneliness, my lacks or not-good-enoughness.

3 Are you and this personality getting along well or not?

This personality has been a barrier to living authentically and the life I want. I see Disconnected Jenny show up at Korean drama series binge watching sessions.

4 What do you want to do about it at this juncture?

I will say "hi" to Disconnected Jenny, accept my vulnerabilities, and choose an alternative way to show up, such as Self-compassionate Jenny.

I-DO-NOT-NEED-IT JENNY

1 When and where do you see this personality?

When I want something, and I do not get to have it, I-Do-Not-Need-It Jenny shows up with resignation, and hides my true desire or need.

2 What does it do for you? (hide/seek/show up/etc.)

Cover up my disappointment.

3 Are you and this personality getting along well or not?

I-Do-Not-Need-It Jenny and I do not get along well. This Jenny suppresses my real needs (e.g. deep down, I hope to be heard, seen or understood).

 4 What do you want to do about it at this juncture?

To acknowledge what I need, and find a way to fulfill this need because I am enough and I deserve to meet my need.

MISUNDERSTOOD JENNY

1 When and where do you see this personality?

When I interact with someone I trust, and he/she misunderstands me.

2 What does it do for you? (hide/seek/show up/etc.)

Misunderstood Jenny makes me feel sad that others can not get my real intentions, and misunderstand me. I may want to cling to my thoughts of why others can't understand, and I want to explain myself persistently. At times, others may not be able to provide me the space or opportunity to explain, and I may come from fear of wanting to clear things up.

3 Are you and this personality getting along well or not?

Misunderstood Jenny and I do not get along well, but I am aware of this personality and hold space for this Jenny.

4 What do you want to do about it at this juncture?

Trust myself, and give myself a sense of security. I can then bring back Calm Jenny and ask others if they would have room for me to offer an alternative perspective.

1 When and where do you see this personality?

When I was younger, I did and said things that pleased others (e.g., to be a good girl).

PEOPLE-PLEASING JENNY

2 What does it do for you? (hide/seek/show up/etc.)

People-pleasing Jenny sacrificed my authenticity to be liked, loved, and cared for.

3 Are you and this personality getting along well or not?

I felt conflicted from within. I was laughing with others from outside, while doubting myself from inside.

4 What do you want to do about it at this juncture?

People-pleasing Jenny is now being archived, not forgotten, but to be kept and thanked for how she was trying to "protect me" from being "abandoned." This was all my perceived threat when I did not know better and thought it was real.

In my relationship, here is an example of how my personality shows up. My husband and I focus on child-rearing for most of our daily life, on top of work demands. We make sure Ally has her basic survival needs met, including meals, pocket money to buy food in the canteen, savings for the future, ironed school uniforms, a clean and cozy home environment, chauffeuring her to school and lessons, and more. Over and above that, we are also providing her a structure so that she does not neglect her physical, social, emotional, and cognitive development. By "a structure" I am referring to giving her learning opportunities and space to build the skills. For instance, my husband was an athlete during his adolescent years; hence, he tends to pay more attention to Ally's physical development and gives her the opportunity to be exposed to tae kwon do, track and field, etc. Thankfully, Ally enjoys these physical activities without much resistance. As a conscious parent, I pay attention to Ally's social-emotional development, observe her nature and temperament, and identify her strengths and weaknesses. As consciously as I can, without having me getting in her way, I give her opportunities to make her own decisions, and provide her safe space to express her emotions such as frustrations with peers, so that she can learn how to regulate her own emotions from sad to calm.[7] If not, I allow Ally to have the space and time to feel her uncomfortable emotions and then decide a way to ease herself from there. This is usually what *Calm Jenny* does well.

---

7   Nonjudgmental and empathetic listening. I expand this in CARE Method in Chapter 7.

It usually leaves us very little time for each other as a couple. I can see *Disconnected Jenny* crawling out without hesitation. I would bury myself in front of the TV or work some more, instead of trying to make time for my husband and I to catch up and check in with one another on how our day went. Hence, I can easily neglect spending time with him. Because I am aware of my different personalities and what each of them does for me, with mindfulness, I can observe and catch myself for not staying as *Disconnected Jenny*, and take a different action.

I highly recommend you become an inquisitive collector of your own different personalities, so that you can keep a distance from yourself and get to learn more about yourself as a close friend. I have also collected my child's different personalities. At times, they come in handy and help me to decide in different situations at that moment to support her as a coach, observer, or friend. I will discuss more in Chapter 7 when we go through ways to support your child using the CARE Method.

Conscious Self-Parenting and Reflection

Album of Your Personalities Exercise
Let us do an exercise on observing yourself for a week (in fact, this may be a lifelong exercise) and to collect a list of personalities you see yourself put on.

Album of Your *Child's Personalities Exercise*

Let us do an exercise on observing your child for a week (in fact, this may be a lifelong exercise) and to collect a list of personalities you see your child put on.

OVERLY EXCITED ALLY

1 When and where do you see this personality?

When she is doing new things or things she likes to do (e.g., taking a roller coaster ride or going for a holiday trip).

2 What does it do for him or her? (hide/seek/show up/etc.)

She is showing up for her aliveness.

3 Are you or your child and this personality of your child getting along well or not?

For me, I like this personality, and she is full of energy.

For her, she enjoys herself very much, sometimes to the extent that she does not know how to stop; hence, she needs to be reminded to rest.

4 How would you help your child to get to know more about this personality at this juncture?

Keep, but remind her in advance to contain herself and keep herself safe. I can also bring in a past incident where she was overly excited during a theme park visit and refused to wear an extra layer of jacket during wintertime. On the very same night, she was worn out, caught a cold, and had a fever.

THE EVER-EVOLVING SELF

When pain gets triggered, it also means our childhood wound is pressed on; our unmet needs from childhood would require a considerable amount of time and effort to heal. In fact, the psychological wounds may not go away and be healed entirely, and some of the old wounds can be retriggered along the way, even if we are on our healing path. Each healing can give you new awareness on alternative ways to deal with the pain in a healthier and more productive manner. As a virtuous cycle is repeating itself, you are transforming the "pain*full*" experience toward a resilient and "pain*less*" one, or when you are curious and determined, you may have an opportunity to advance your spiritual quest.

The following is my own unchaining or healing journey through self-parenting; it feels like upward moving spiral growth as I look back, similar to the koru pattern.[8] During this unchaining from the old patterns process, through the meditation practices and dance therapy sessions, I constantly remind myself to go back to my true self, connecting with my true self by first feeling my aliveness through every breath I take, every move I make, every heartbeat I feel. Embracing my pure being. From my pure being, I then connect with my mind that interprets the meaning or purpose of my aliveness. The following picture and table show the stages of my ever-evolving self-growth and awakening process. It starts from self-discovery through feeling trapped with emotional pain or suffering, I called it the Stage o.

---

8   Koru is a spiral shape based on the appearance of a new unfurling silver fern frond. It symbolizes new life, growth, strength, and peace. Its shape "conveys the idea of perpetual movement," while the inner coil "suggests returning to the point of origin." Source: Te Ara: The Encyclopedia of New Zealand, s.v., "the koru."

Unchaining Yourself from Old Patterns and Progressing toward Continuous Self-Growth

The Ever-Evolving Self & Continuous Self-Growth—From "Feeling Pain from Within" to "Self-Transcendence"
(See also previous diagram)

Stage 0: "I Feel (Emotional) Pain" *Egoic self with recurring self-judgment and negative self-talk*	Stage 1: Self-Acceptance *From stuck to surrender*	Stage 2: Self-Trust *From doubt/discomfort to trust/safety*	Stage 3: Self-Compassion *From shame to compassion*	Stage 4: Self-Resiliency *From "beating around the bush" to courage*	Stage N: Self-Transcendence *From self to oneness*
Identify habitual patterns that do not serve you. →	I am stuck. →	I doubt myself. →	I do not deserve love. →	What now? Numb/Hide/Resist/Appease others again? →	I honor my being in this world; I do not have to do (and do endlessly) to prove myself. →
Identify and label your different personalities, especially those you are not getting along with well. →	I accept life is ever-changing.	I avoid responsibilities.	I unknot my resistance. →	Courageous me to confront my old patterns due to a triggered inner child/childhood wound →	I have unchained myself and reclaimed my aliveness. →
Curiously interested in finding ways to get rid of the painful trapped state.	I surrender.	I am responsible for my thinking/feeling/actions. →	I feel loved. →	Resilient me →	I can be selfless and blend in with Mother Earth as one.
		I got this. →	I can love others how I want to be loved and am ready to help others.	Face it, show up, and move on once more.	
		I trust myself.			

From Stage 0 to Stage 1, 2, or 3

When you are overwhelmed by discomfort or anxiety, you may start finding ways to get rid of the painful trapped state. At times, you may be stuck (Stage 1) at first, then you tell yourself that you cannot fight too hard when you get stuck; you will then surrender to the as-is. Other times, you may doubt yourself, and then you may avoid owning your responsibilities that led you to where you are (Stage 2), then you may gradually gain trust from yourself and say, "Yes, I got this." At some other times, you may think you are unworthy of love (Stage 3). At the beginning you may have been resisting this thought of saying, "I am not enough," etc. To transform from that state, you will need to be ready to trust and tell yourself, "I got this. I can do this!" Instead of telling yourself you are not good enough, you shift from shame to compassion with self-love.

These stages may come and go like a vicious cycle, and the pattern keeps repeating itself. There will be times you may not get to the last few positive shifts within each stage. Or if you do get to the other end of a positive shift, you may find it hard to stay grounded and rooted consistently. At this point, resourceful you may start discovering alternative ways to heal your emotional pain, or you may also refer to some of the effective ways I have experienced and shared in Chapter 2. As you are taking time and working hard in this healing process, such as integrating meditation and mindfulness into your daily routines, you can gradually and steadily build up your "observer" muscle.

You can then be aware of your different personalities who are showing up, and attend to these personalities' needs, and you may tap into different techniques and methods to bring yourself back to your calming state or rooted self. Little by little, you may enter Stage 4, Self-Resiliency.

Stage 4: Self-Resiliency

You may observe your old patterns reappearing. This time around, you are courageous and experienced in dealing with your emotional pain. At this stage, you may see yourself as the author of your life, and not a victim; hence, you have the clarity on how you want to maneuver your way out.

Stage N: Self-Transcendence

Self-transcendence is one of the human qualities among compassion, conscience, and will to meaning, according to Viktor Frankl:

> Most psychological disorders result from failing to meet our basic spiritual need for meaning, as a result of egotistically pursuing happiness and success based on misguided values. Paradoxically, healing and well-being, to a large extent, require a shift away from attachment to materialistic pursuits to the spiritual realm of self-detachment and self-transcendence. The essence of logotherapy is to awaken people's sense of responsibility to fulfill a concrete meaning in their existence.[9]

9   Cuncic, "What to Know about Logotherapy"; Wong, "Meaning-Seeking."...

In fact, self-transcendence is also mentioned in Maslow's Hierarchy of Needs pyramid as the final stage. Maslow has provided a comprehensive definition:

> Transcendence refers to the very highest and most inclusive or holistic levels of human consciousness, behaving and relating, as ends rather than as means, to oneself, to significant others, to human beings in general, to other species, to nature, and to the cosmos.[10]

From the very beginning of my personal growth and awakened journey, I was feeling lost and doubtful about my existence in this world. With the victim mindset, I was trapped inside my emotional pain and unconsciously allowed myself to delve into a sense of self-helplessness. I wanted to hang on to the cliff edge, and I was finding ways to save myself from falling. Words from wisdom teachers healed me again and again, and they awakened my inner wisdom and strength. I started to accept myself and found light that gave me hope to give a meaning to my existence. My inner voice started to reflect, *Perhaps all things that happened in the past happened for a reason; I may be able to make a difference with my existence.* Having exposed myself to wise words that connected with me, I tried different ways to

---

...The notion of logotherapy was created with the Greek word logos ("meaning"). Frankl's concept is based on the premise that the primary motivational force of an individual is to find meaning in life.

10 Maslow, *Farther Reaches of Human Nature*, 279.

heal my wounded inner child. I could feel that my emotional love tank was filling up little by little. [11] I could trust myself a little more through the healing process, applying those practices, methods, and approaches. Letting go of my shame, I could give love and compassion to myself. Because I get to know more about myself and experience self-love, I can then love my child unselfishly (i.e., not asking her to love me back unconsciously). After all, she was the one who helped me experience unconditional love first, sparking my awakened journey.

Along the way, some of the emotional pain revisited me, and I was a little shocked and frustrated at first, as I thought I was healed. From there, I have also learned that these childhood wounds would show up in other forms and sizes, and they may not be completely healed. However, I become more resilient to face them. As I have also picked up dance/movement therapy, I can feel my connection with myself has deepened. My child and I are one; my family and I are one; my community and I are one; the planet and I are one; the universe and I are one.

From self to unself, feel the oneness. This mind-body-soul connection allows you to experience and honor the sense of oneness with Mother Earth. Your existence of just being you on this planet is enough, and you are enough; you are whole and complete. You are home from within and are connected to Mother Earth as one. At this state, a sense of love and gratitude flows

---

11   "Emotional love tank" is a term coined by Gary Chapman and Ross Campbell in their 2016 book, *The 5 Love Languages of Children*.

through your body. As you take action, creativity is in the flow, which is an expression of your aliveness. With the presence of heart and clarity of your being, your mind-body-soul connectedness gives you strength and firm inner alignment. The negative, doubtful, or judgmental noises within and around you are powerless. Your existence is worthy, as are people and all living things and nature around you. You are one with the universe, and this interconnectedness and evolving consciousness has given you and I a deeper and greater sense of belongingness and responsibilities to be there for each other, which includes the one and only planet we are living on.

In this self-transcendence journey, you may transform from sympathy (the stage where ego or false self may be stuck in one's own pain, and understand others are also suffering) to empathy (the stage where one is releasing or embracing ego or false self and protective layers and may tune into and share others' pain and suffering) to compassion (the stage where one connects with true self, and is compassionate towards the self and others, feels others' pain because of one's own pain, and wants to help). And eventually, to unself, to unite with the higher consciousness (the stage where there are no separations between you, ecosystem, Mother Earth, universe and I, and we are all one universe. Your breath and body become the proof of your aliveness and existence, pain becomes inevitable and is part of the flow of aliveness), and no longer limited by one's self.

I have gotten a taste of the self-transcendence stage when I am pursuing my spiritual growth with a wisdom teacher, spiritual guide and practitioner Sola. In fact, spiritual growth was not my initial intention to follow Sola's teaching; I was pursuing my self-discovery and my truth, getting closer to my true self. Among all the wisdom learnings and meditation practices I have learned from Sola for the last two years, moments of my integrated self with the universe as one—not just from knowing or understanding it, but having awareness and getting into the unself state while experiencing it through my body—was profound. When I am in the state of unself, a sense of inclusiveness spreads within me; compassion is a way of interacting with others. Through unself, no "me" or "I" gets in the way; oneness respects all life, embraces all walks of life, all states of awareness, all experiences, and all feelings.

Pain is indeed the portal of transformation; how deep or how far you wish to transform, you get to decide.

WHY BOTHER TO REEXPOSE THE OLD WOUNDS

For more than fifteen years, Caroline Myss, author of *Why People Don't Heal and How They Can*, studied why some people heal while others do not. She pointed out that "After experiencing a traumatic or tragic experience, these people tend to look at every new experience through the lens of the wound it inflicted on them." She further elaborated, "Although this state of mind is sad, self-limiting, and defeatist, some people derive great power in maintaining it because it gives permission to lead a life of minimum expectation and limited responsibility.

It allows them to lean on others for assistance and to play on their guilt to keep that assistance coming."[12] I was intrigued and confronted by this new perspective she brought into my own interpretation of *I healed from my wounds; therefore, others would want to have the same experience and heal theirs too.* Bringing this perspective in for your consideration, if you happened to get stuck by "why you should bother to reexpose the old wounds," I would like to invite you to be curiously interested in having these possibilities being present to you. For example, you have the freedom to choose your authentic self-expression. When encountering challenges, you get in touch with your inner strength and authentic power, and you know that you can decide when you are ready to bounce back from setbacks, usually within a short period of time—or even to have additional options for you to choose the kind of life you would like to have. At the very last breath of our life, we get to smile and say to ourselves, "So glad to be here."

STAND FIRM IN YOUR TRUTH

On a family outing, my husband brought Ally and me to a reservoir, and there, a tall and nature-decorated cotton tree captured both Ally's and my eyes. I did not know what tree it was until Ally told me it was a cotton tree. She then picked up some fallen cotton from the ground, and I took photos of the tree.

---

12   Myss, *Why People Don't Heal and How They Can*, 31–32.

It brought the two of us so much joy. For Ally, it was the fluffy cotton, but for me, it was the tree's standing-tall state that attracted me, as well as the leaves that went around the tree trunk. Those leaves went around the white tree trunk just like a necklace on a lady's neck. Maybe it was those decorative leaves that let me see myself in that tree.

Beautiful Rooted Tree That Stands Strongly for Our Children and People around Us

Five years ago, I started breaking free, and today, the image I have of myself, after shedding my layers of egoic self—the wanting-to-prove-to-others-that-I-was-worthy me—is a cotton tree. I stand firmly and beautifully for my inner child and the people around me.

Now a strong voice from within says, *I have something to say, and I am worthy of being listened to.* This purpose I discovered for myself was rooted deeply, and now it has been revealed.

How do you know you have reached this stage? You have clarity in your mind; your heart is pounding steadily without energetic blockages; and your body is functioning in the flow of life without much aching.

Your life has changed in the following ways:

- Life is not as difficult as it once seemed to be.
- Goals seem achievable.
- Human relationships are not as intimidating as before.
- Time seems easier to manage.
- Life has meaning.
- Not only do I feel a new sense of freedom, but my being is connected with Mother Earth as one, and I am ready to show up with the oneness as an earth mother.

Clarity is power. Life becomes clearer through knowing yourself more.

Conscious Self-Parenting and Reflection

When was the last time you felt grateful for your existence? What happened that sparked that gratitude?

No pain. No gain. No growth. See pain as an opportunity for you to get in touch with your inner strength, and to rediscover and get closer to your true self. Take the invitation of pain to be curiously interested in finding out what is hidden within you, and start your awakening journey through adapting the healing methods that suit you.

As you have shifted your perception about yourself along this healing journey, do continue to be compassionate toward yourself; befriend your egoic voices that would want you to go back to your pain and old patterns. You can thank these egoic voices for doing their best to protect you; however, let them know they no longer serve you and that you have found your way to authentic power, to reclaim your sovereignty to be, to do, to feel you—your true self. Have fun observing how the awakened you is navigating the conscious relationships with you, your loved ones, and people around you.

four

CONSCIOUS RELATIONSHIPS

B efore I started my conscious self-parenting journey, heal-ing my inner child, I was someone who would sit at the dinner table listening to my dad and youngest sister's conversation with others, putting a smile on my face, nodding my head, and feeling lonely deep inside. I love my parents and siblings; however, I just felt I was oddly not able to fit in from where I was internally. I was working hard to fit in from out-side by putting a smile on my face. I was surely there listening with politeness, but I would feel more relaxed when I got home. After I learned to be my own observer through mindfulness and meditation, I got to understand that I was "working too hard." I was too busy trying to fit in by "making" myself seem like a good and polite listener, and I forgot about myself, what I valued most, and my own needs.

I learned that my presence can be relaxed and at ease. As I have found my value and self-worth, I feel comfortable in my own skin sitting at the dinner table. I know I can choose to be there in whichever state I am in at the present moment. I know very well the reason I am at the dinner table, as I want to spend quality time with my family members; I love them and they love my presence. That is all I know. I can choose to join or not join the conversations depending on the topic, and there is nothing wrong with that. Because I can be at peace with the above, there may be stories and events that pop up that I can share, and I become less lonely and yet contribute to the conversations at dinner. To maintain my authentic presence, I just need to keep breathing, bring myself back to the present moment, and let go of my negative self-talk or distractive self-judgment. It gets easier and quicker as one masters the mindfulness practice coupled with breathing technique over time. At the same time, going through the healing process described in Chapter 3 will help you to get closer to yourself, and to be comfortable in your own skin. You will enjoy your being more and accept the perfectly imperfect you. This helps ease your own judgmental thoughts in a social setting.

FIVE KEYS TO MAINTAINING
CONSCIOUS RELATIONSHIPS

Here are five keys to maintaining conscious relationships with your loved ones:

1. Mindfully check in with your inner alignment.
2. Be a conscious observer of your thinking/feeling/doing.
3. Practice mindful listening to your child or your loved ones in front of you, and listen to your inner voices.
4. Hold space for your authenticity to embrace your emotion at the moment.
5. Insert conscious pauses and choose your action or response.

Your Inner Alignment

To have clarity of your *why*, understand why you do what you do.

Kira Newman, managing editor of the Greater Good Science Center at the University of California, Berkeley, shared this about a research study:

> A group of Australian researchers surveyed more than 800 people, mostly undergraduate students, about their levels of mindfulness, well-being, and "values-based action."
>
> Values-based action reflects how much progress you're making toward the things that matter to you—your goals, self-improvement, and purpose in life—and how much you

get distracted or discouraged along the way. For example, if you value compassion, you would rate yourself higher if you took time out of a busy week to check on friends who are struggling. The mindfulness measured here was participants' ability to stay focused, minimize distraction, and avoid judging their thoughts and feelings.

In their analysis, the researchers found that more mindful people had higher well-being—with much of this link accounted for by their acting more in line with their values.[1]

According to the Greater Good Science Center, "Mindfulness means maintaining a moment-by-moment awareness of our thoughts, feelings, bodily sensations, and surrounding environment, through a gentle, nurturing lens. Mindfulness also involves acceptance, meaning that we pay attention to our thoughts and feelings without judging them."[2]

The more I practice to be present in the moment, and the more I become less judgmental about myself, the more I am able to accept myself and who I am. This opens up space for me to notice my inner world such as my thoughts, feelings, and body sensations while receiving information from the surrounding environment and observing my interaction with people such as my child. Because I value authenticity, when I am interacting with my child, the inner alignment of how I think

1   Newman, "Can Mindfulness Help You Be More Authentic?"
2   *Greater Good Magazine*, "What Is Mindfulness?"

and feel allows me to speak my truth. This mind-body-heart alignment strengthens the trust within me and radiates the true expression of my integrated being. You may also refer to the "Bring Me Home" section in Chapter 6.

Be a Conscious Observer

Before I become an observer of myself, I practice Vipassana meditation (or insight meditation) to strengthen my muscle to consciousness. I follow multiple wisdom teachers, including Dr. Shefali Tsabary, who uses meditation as her main pathway to wisdom. She integrated Western psychology, Eastern philosophy (i.e., Chinese Laozi's *Tao Te Ching*), and Indian Vipassana meditation into her courses. You can set up a daily routine and practice meditation or write reflective journal entries to explore your inner wounds or inner resources. It allows you as a parent to be more aware of your own thoughts, feelings, and actions. As you discover who you are, your actions will become more value-based. For instance, you value kindness as you get to know who you are and what you value most in life. You may start focusing on doing things that show kindness to others; you may give up your seat to those who need it more during a public transport ride; you may lend your hand and give your time to help a visually impaired person to cross the road. You will be less distracted by demands or things that do not align with your values. Your actions are more connected with who you are. You realize there is no longer a need to trade your authenticity for approval or please others.

My first taste of being a conscious parent was when I was able to detach and observe my thoughts, feelings, and actions as a third party—an observer. When I faced my own emotional reactivity, or how I could support my daughter for her growth, I was able to pause and decide where I would like to land both my daughter and myself. Would it be from the place of love or fear?

I would like to invite you to observe your reactivity. When was the last time you just could not contain your emotions and you were out of control, and at that moment, you just did not know what it was, and you only realized after you had lost your cool? This could be an area you could be curiously interested in exploring deeper and taking opportunities to heal "it." "It" would be your wounded inner child whose needs were unmet, who did not feel seen and heard by your parents or caregivers during childhood. This wounded inner child might have experienced negligence or trauma or emotional pains, and you were longing for security and love.[3] The detachment of your emotional pains will help you see your real child for who he or she is, and not project the child inside you. As you integrate meditation practice in your daily routine, you can strengthen your

3   "Trauma is a psychic wound that hardens you psychologically that then interferes with your ability to grow and develop. It pains you and now you're acting out of pain. It induces fear and now you're acting out of fear. Trauma is not what happens to you, it's what happens inside you as a result of what happened to you. Trauma is that scarring that makes you less flexible, more rigid, less feeling and more defended," explained by Dr. Gabor Maté in "Dr. Gabor Maté on Childhood Trauma."

mindfulness muscle and be a natural observer of inner (as discussed previously in the section "Your Inner Alignment") and outer world (e.g., your surrounding environment and people).

Mindful Listening

Mindful listening is the listening in the presence of the heart. When I practice mindful listening, I am aware of my inner voices and can still mindfully listen to my child or my loved ones in front of me. I am able to bring my meditation state naturally and be present while listening to the other(s).

What do you do in mindful listening? Here is how Chade-Meng Tan described it in his book *Search Inside Yourself*:

As you listen, give your full attention to the speaker. If you find your attention wandering away, just very gently bring it back to the speaker, as if he or she is a sacred object of meditation. As much as possible, try to refrain from speaking, asking questions, or leading the speaker. Remember, you are giving him or her the valuable gift of airtime. You may acknowledge with facial expressions, or by nodding your head, or by saying, "I see," or "I understand," but try not to over-acknowledge so as to not lead the speaker. If the speaker runs out of things to say, give him or her space for silence, and then be available to listen when he or she speaks again.[4]

---

4   Tan, *Search Inside Yourself*, 59.

Conscious Self-Parenting and Reflection

- Let us apply mindfulness when you are interacting with your loved ones, such as your child. You may also try mindful listening. Listen to your child with a nonjudgmental mind. Notice when your mind and attention start wandering away; again, with a nonjudgmental mind, just bring your attention back gently.
- Pen down what you observe about yourself:
  - What do you say to yourself in your mind when you notice your mind wandering away?
  - Is it easy to bring your attention back gently? What helps or does not help you in practicing mindful listening?

Embracing Your Feelings

"Why are we easily triggered emotionally?"

Have you ever asked this question? Or have you ever noticed your excessive consumption of food, alcohol, or television after getting triggered? If you have read Chapter 3, you may be able to relate triggers to childhood or past wounds. Someone or something happened that presses on this wound; therefore, you feel pain. When we can be more aware of our emotional reactivity, and even identify the root cause of our emotional reactivity, we will not be easily subjugated by our feelings. Yes, the root cause is usually related to childhood wounds or our egoic self, who can be defensive when facing "perceived threats" and wants to be right.

Furthermore, as you are strengthening your mindfulness practice, you may become more aware of your inner dialogues, so that your true adult self can stand firmly and tell your egoic self to step aside.

These dialogues may go like this:

- "I own my own peace. You (the other) are just reflecting back a piece of my unease from within. I am curious about why this happens. Let me find out more."

- "I will not be easily affected by you (the other) shouting and yelling at me, and I know my ego wants me to fight back and 'escalate' it to the next level to show my 'power' and how 'good' I can be in fighting back. I want to be seen as the stronger one. I am stronger not because I am fearful of what happened but because I am rooted and able to stay calm from the place of love."

- "I will not let you take away my peace because you want to make me feel bad about how I am not good enough or I am lacking. I can see through *you* (my ego)."

I am not saying that the ego is wrong.

As Eckhart Tolle explained in his book *A New Earth*, "The ego isn't wrong; it's just unconscious. When you observe the ego in yourself, you are beginning to go beyond it. Don't take the ego too seriously... Above all, know that the ego isn't personal. It isn't who you are."[5]

Because I have come to terms with myself and built a healthy relationship with myself, I have gotten in touch with my authenticity and learned to embrace my feelings and own them. This enables me to build and hold conscious relationships with my loved ones, friends, clients, and people around me.

Conscious Pause

To be able to make a conscious pause before reacting to the people you are communicating with helps tremendously with realigning your values-based action or response.

These days, when I do make a mistake due to a slip in inserting a pause before my emotional reactivity, I will first pay attention to my emotional or physiological states (e.g., "I am upset right now") and check my heart rate, breathing rate, body temperature, chest constriction, etc. I will then show up in front of my daughter, apologize to her, and share with her what I or both of us can do differently next time.

At this point, you may get a good picture of how mindfulness plays an important role among the five keys, and how these five keys are intertwined. The following are some examples of how

---

5   Tolle, *A New Earth*, 42.

these keys played out in my conscious relationships with my loved ones. Because of these keys, I get to build a stronger and closer relationship with myself. Furthermore, my relationships with my loved ones also reflect how well I am doing in my own self-parenting, because these relationships are projections or mirrors of my inner world.

OUR RELATIONSHIPS WITH OUR CHILDREN

How do you know you are a conscious parent? Becoming a conscious parent is a progressive journey. Here I am sharing my journey from being a controlling parent to becoming a conscious parent. I was once a controlling parent, who held much guilt inside of me because I was focusing on what I did or did not do in the past, such as spending little time with my child or not signing my child up early enough to learn a third language, etc. When I was not in my guilty mode, I was an anxious parent who was focusing on what had not happened, and making assumptions of what my child would become if she did or did not do things that would "definitely" (in my imaginative mind) impact her future. Hence, I ought to be highly involved in scheduling and structuring her time to shape her into the ideal child in my mind, so that she would struggle less in the future. If you agree with what I did and did not do as a controlling mother, now is a good time to take my invitation to be curiously interested in self-parenting. Try connecting with yourself through mindfulness practice and check in with your emotional triggers that bring you straight into reactivity that creates a disconnection between you and your children. At the end of the day, all parents have good intentions when it comes to raising and nurturing our children. It is about time to review what has not been working well for you in your parenting journey and to be open-minded to alternative parenting methods that may bring you and your children healthy growth, joy, and inner peace.

Before I share how I continue to grow as a conscious parent and hold a conscious relationship with my child, allow me to share some of my early days parenting, and how I parented my child from an unconscious space.

The Controlling Mother in Me

When my daughter was eleven years old, she would remind me of the time I hit her palm when she was three, the only time I used physical punishment. I had yet to hear of Conscious Parenting, but I knew about managing my child's behaviors using the ABC model:

- Antecedent: the events, actions, or circumstances that occur before a behavior
- Behavior: the behavior
- Consequences: the action or response that follows the behavior

Our responses should always focus on strengthening desired behavior, promoting the use of the replacement behavior, and decreasing the occurrence of the problem behavior. An important aspect of this prospect is understanding those responses or consequences that maintain, and either enhance or decrease, behavior over time.[6]

She said she could still feel the pain in her hand. What happened was I bought a high-end pricey floor mat for her, and she doodled on it, and it was a new and expensive piece. I got mad, and I hit her palm three times. I was hoping that by giving her three hits on her palm as a response to her doodling at inappropriate places, she would learn her lesson and decrease this undesirable behavior. If I did pause and ask myself why she would doodle on the new mat, I would not choose the same response or consequence. Three-year-old Ally might also be as excited as I was seeing this new mat, and she expressed her curiosity by doodling on this colorful mat. And of course, she would not understand what a high-end pricey floor mat meant at that age.

Looking back, what was missing then was to insert *conscious pause*. If I probe further about why I hit her palm, I think I was feeling regretful for not seeing that coming in advance, and feeling upset with myself for not taking preventive action in time. In fact, my biggest regret now is hitting her palm due to my own emotional reactivity. What I could do differently back then would be to tell her what to do and not to do on the mat. Being a conscious parent and practicing mindfulness, taking pauses as an

6   Pratt and Dubie, "Observing Behavior Using A-B-C Data."

observer can help me realign my values-based action. As I value connection with my child, I can pause, think, and choose my action (i.e., give a more child-centric response or consequence). Otherwise, my emotional reactivity ("I am upset") would run its short circuit and lead to undesirable outcomes (i.e., my child still remembers I hit her three times in her palm many years later, and she thought she was a bad kid). As soon as I noticed my emotional or physiological states, in this case, my heart rate went faster and my cheeks felt warm. I could take a few deep breaths, calm myself down, and adjust my inner alignment.

Conscious Self-Parenting and Reflection

- Are you aware of your emotional triggers? What are they? What past event prompted your triggers?
- Have you ever felt a time where you could not break free from your strong negative emotion, such as anger or jealousy, taking over you? How did you manage to get out of it? If you did not manage to get out of it, try this next time: you can shift your awareness and pay attention to your emotional or physiological states by placing your right hand over your heart and placing your left hand over your hara (below your navel or belly button); gently apply some pressure on both spaces. From here, take a few deep breaths to calm yourself down.

As a conscious parent, I can see the "controlling mother" in me showed up in different times, spaces, and forms while parenting Ally. This time around it was my fear that got in my way. One night at 10:25, eleven-year-old Ally was playing an online game with her friend. I texted her to find out what time she promised to end the online game. She said she did not promise. I asked again what time she set for herself to end as part of her self-care commitment. She did not reply. I observed my anxiety from within. I felt pain in my heart. My inner voices started:

Controlling Jenny: Should I walk into her room and ask her?
Calming Jenny: Should I give her some space to practice how to end the game on her own?

I could feel side-by-side emotions surface (i.e., feeling anxious and trying to stay calm at the same time). My heart continued to ache. I ran out of ideas to remind her; I felt lost. On one hand, I wanted to give her an opportunity to face consequences; on the other hand, I could feel how much I wanted to control and shorten her time playing online games. I checked in with myself and asked, "Why did it trigger me when I did not receive a response from her?" "Ally was so rude when she read the messages and did not respond!" "What did I make it mean?" At this moment, I could not attune to her needs, I noticed. I realized I made it mean that I was not as important as her friend, and I was not a good enough mom who could help her build up good online gaming habits. At the end, I did knock on her door, and

I requested her to check my message, as she was still in the middle of playing an online game with her friend. After a short while, she ended the game, read my message, and explained to me that she did not get a notification of my message and apologized for not ending the game earlier.

Could you identify the keys of self-parenting I could have used when I noticed the controlling mother in me? Yes, I could "be a conscious observer," "embrace my feelings authentically," and "insert conscious pauses and choose my action or response."

Staying Conscious to Your Child's Strengths

One night during our bedtime conversations, while ten-year-old Ally was sharing what happened in school, I could listen to her attentively and allow her to exhibit her strength (i.e., she is an observant child):

> Ally: Mommy, it was so strange to watch myself in the classroom today. As usual, I saw myself raising my hand to answer a question the teacher asked, and I saw another classmate was doing so too. His eagerness to answer the question reminded me to check if I was doing the same.
>
> Me: So what did you observe? Were you the same as the classmate?
>
> Ally: Teacher did choose me to answer the question. As I put down my hand and answered her question, I

realized I was not feeling proud, even though the classmates were all looking at me with admiring eyes.

Ally (giving me an honest look): I did not do it to get attention from them. I did it for me because I really wanted to answer the question.

Later, I summed up what she observed by pointing out how observant she was about herself, and what I liked about her observation. I gave her affirmation on her ability to differentiate her intention of raising her hand and responding to a question. She could sense and feel that she did not raise her hand so that she could feel proud and show off how smart she was when she got the answer correctly, but to fulfill her own desire to respond to a question and solve a problem as a keen learner.

Conscious Self-Parenting and Reflection

Have you tried observing yourself in the mirror exercise in Chapter 1? If not, please try it out now before doing the following exercise with your child.

Invite Your Child to Join You in Observing Oneself in the Mirror
After you have experienced the observing yourself in the mirror exercise, you may have a sense of whether your child will be open to joining you in this exercise. I would

recommend doing this with children aged seven and above. For younger children, they are still in the developmental stage in forming self-awareness.[7]

You may invite your child and share with him or her that the intent of the exercise is to have a taste of self-observation in the mirror. You may explain the flow of the exercise, and he or she will observe himself or herself in the mirror for three minutes. Each of you will do it in front of a mirror; you may do it together if you have multiple mirrors, or you may take turns to do this. Sharing the same mirror is not preferred, as you and your child may get distracted during the process. Your child gets to say yes or no to join this exercise, and you must accept their response. You may try to invite him or her again next time.

For our children, we can give a simpler instruction, as the focus is to give them a taste of observing themselves in the mirror, to help them to reflect on what they have observed. Here is an example of the instructions. You may tell your child:

1. Let us set a three-minute timer.
2. Observe different parts of your body in the mirror. You may start paying attention to your whole face: your facial features such as eyebrows, eyes, nose, lips, cheeks, ears, and other parts of your body.
3. For older children, pay attention to your facial muscles. Sense and feel them. Are they relaxed or tight? Slowly and gently, transition to mindful listening, and listen

---

7   Krisch, "Five Stages of Self-Awareness." That is a mirror (Level 1); there is a person in it (Level 2); that person is me (Level 3); that person is going to be me forever (Level 4); and everyone else can see it (Level 5).

to your thoughts; If you like, make a mental note about your thoughts.

4. Repeat the above.

5. Stop when the timer is up.

During the debrief, you may apply mindful listening and listen to their internal self-talk, if any. Is their internal self-talk geared toward positivity or negativity? Additionally, you can also listen from the strengths of your child's observation of himself or herself in the mirror. Say she notices her body sensation, feelings, thoughts, or more, and she is able to describe them through words—well done. Praise her effort in observing herself gently or closely or open-mindedly, etc. Ask how she finds this exercise, and what her overall experience is like in observing herself in the mirror.

Because you have started practicing mindfulness, you can be ready to actively identify your child's strengths through mindful and nonjudgmental listening, and attune to who your child is as a deep conscious observer.

Embracing Your Genuine Feelings while Having Difficult Conversations with Your Child

One night, nine-year-old Ally and I talked about what would happen if one day she could no longer have daily conversations with me. Immediately, I could feel side-by-side emotions within me: on one hand, I was very thankful about how Ally would miss me and cherish our relationship at that moment.

On the other hand, I was feeling sad to talk about my death or departure from this lifetime, and how I would no longer be able to be there for her when she needed me.

Our conversation went like this:

Me: I will always live in your heart even if I will not be physically around with you. You could still talk to me by whispering to your heart.

Ally: Mommy, I would whisper to my heart while I am having inner dialogues with myself. I would be preoccupied with that and would not be able to keep you there.

Me: Which part of your body would remind you of me? Would it be your forehead, as I kissed you there frequently? Or would it be your lips?

Ally (silent and in deep thought): It would be my cheeks.

Me: Next time when you need to talk to me when I am not around physically, you could touch your cheeks and have an inner dialogue with me from there.

Being a conscious mother helps me to be courageous, and yet to be able to connect with my truth, when I face difficult conversations with my child. I was able to embrace my side-by-side emotions and provide mindful listening. I can detach my reactivity, give a pause, adjust my inner alignment, and choose what I want to say authentically and where I want to lead myself and my child toward the completion of our conversation.

Do start taking your values-based action by getting clarity in your *inner alignment*.

Staying Conscious to Your Child's Emotions

Our children are conscious beings. We can help them to see their own natural abilities and inner resources to deal with people and things that happen around them. Here is another example from my interaction with Ally to elaborate further. Another night, eleven-year-old Ally and I were going through her bedtime routine, having a little night chat before bed:

> Ally: Mommy, I cannot seem to get rid of the holey bones image out of my head from the online advertisement we saw just now.
>
> I listen attentively.
>
> Ally: It reminds me of my first dropped tooth that time as I peeped into it. There were holes, and those holes gave me a chilled feeling. They disgusted me.

She was restless, she was rolling to her left and then her right, and shortly after that, she covered herself with a blanket. I took a look at the clock; it was almost eleven o'clock at night. She had to wake up at six thirty in the morning the next day.

At that moment, I heard two inner voices in me:

1. *What was that to make a fuss about? Just go to sleep!*
2. I could see she was a little out of her usual calmness;

I could see her stiff back. *How can I help and support her?* I thought.

Me: Ally, would you like mommy to tell you stories about how you were so courageous in the past to deal with things you did not like or enjoy?

Ally nods her head and shows half of her face from the blanket. I can see her tight eyebrows.

Me: When you were six, we were baking bread, the breadmaker spoiled, and you decided to knead the dough yourself, and you...

Ally (slowly brings down the blanket, keeps it under her arms, and looks at me): Mommy, I am feeling slightly better. Can you help me to stroke and massage my back?

Me: Of course.

As I stroke her back, I can feel her stiff back softening.

Ally: Mommy, I feel better. You know what, Mommy? For the first time, Mommy, you are able to take care of me really well. Good job, Mommy.

Me: Thank you, Ally, for your acknowledgment.

Because I was able to own and embrace my emotion in the first place, I did not take in Ally's anxiety, and provided the space she needed, and she was able to just focus on her own discomfort. At the end, she was able to tune in to her inner resource, and told me what support I could provide her. She could then calm herself down through her own inner knowing of her needs and ask me for appropriate support. Most importantly, she felt safe to articulate her needs without being judged.

I hope you get to see the benefits of owning and embracing your feelings when connecting with your child(ren) during daily interaction. In fact, while your child is tuning into her own inner resources, you are also given space to tap into your own inner resources. You can quiet down the noises in your head and listen to your inner wisdom.

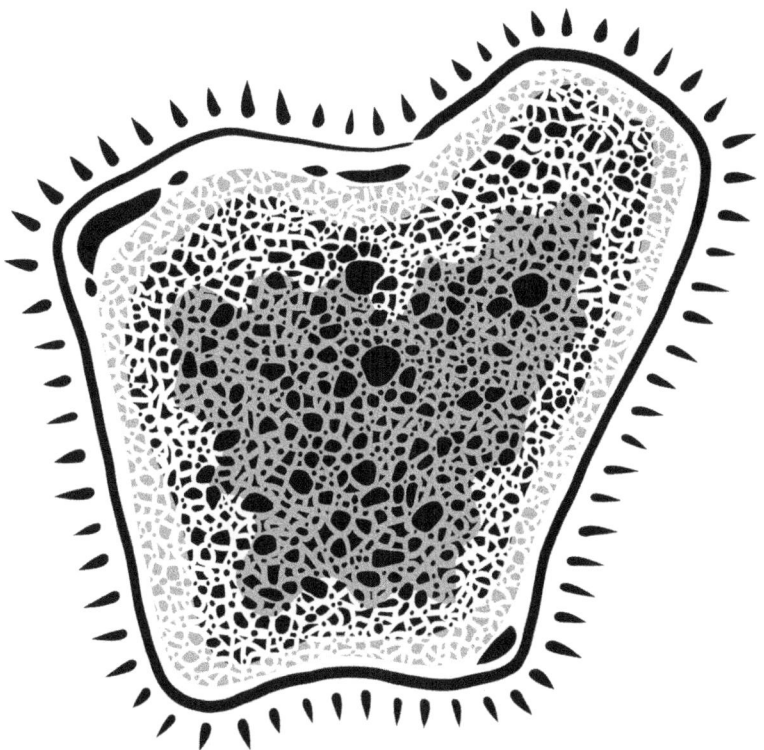

Helping My Child Help Herself while Experiencing Trypophobia

Observing Yourself

My daughter and I love spending time together preparing dinner. When she was nine years old, I showed her how to flip an egg. At the beginning, she chose to watch. After a few times, she told me that she would like to give it a try. I handed the pan over to her, and she started her usual procedure of frying an egg. As she was practicing how to flip it, after I had shown her one more time before her turn, I could tell that she might not be able to flip it over successfully, from the way she held the pan and her flipping gesture and movement. I chose not to say anything and gave her the space to try. I could feel that my heart was pounding a little faster than before, and I had to breathe deeper as I watched her. I had to consciously keep myself calm without saying a word. True enough, when she gathered all her courage to do her first flip, the egg landed on the stove. She immediately said, "I knew it, I could not do this right." I encouraged her and asked her to try another one, and I told her she could give the one that fell on the stove to me. Cleanliness to Ally is a big deal; she would not eat something that was scattered on the table. As parents, we contributed to her perspective, especially my husband, Ally's overprotective father. I was surprised by her reply; she said, "Mommy, it is fine; I will eat this. I was the one who could not flip and catch it on the pan, let me eat it." It felt heartwarming knowing she was bearing the consequence of her action.

Having practiced Conscious Parenting for five to six years now, it does not only help me build a closer and stronger relationship with my child, it also helps me to

- accept myself for who I am and who I am not;
- build closer connection with myself;
- allow my loved ones to be who they are, accept their differences, and not make them wrong;
- create a conscious environment at home for my child and myself that allows us to grow together because I have worked on my own inner child healing; and
- know and follow the boundaries I set for her and myself.

Because I know it takes so much awareness and transformation of pain to get to where I am now, I have more compassion for myself and the parents I serve. With the key that starts my own Conscious Parenting journey, I am able to start to pick up and acknowledge those lessons I have learned, and the way I have made myself wrong constantly has not helped me feel better from my own pains and suffering. I can see my weaknesses, which I hate to accept, but still know that I am whole and complete as who I am even with those weaknesses. Being a conscious parent helps me to be more aware of my heart. I can identify when my ego is speaking louder than my true adult self, trying to get me to operate out of fear. Subsequently, I will be seen as a controlling mother who just wants my child to follow my way. What is it like for you when you are parenting your child? Have you ever told yourself again and again, "I should not say that to him/her," or "I do not like how much I control my child because I do not enjoy being controlled myself." Did you reflect and try to do differently next time?

Conscious Self-Parenting and Reflection

- What are some of the mistakes you think you have made in parenting your child? List them.
- What do you learn from these mistakes? Do you get to know more about your parenting style or yourself through these mistakes or lessons learned?
- How do you feel when you repeat the same mistakes again?
- How do you feel when you are able to take a different action and stop repeating the mistakes?

The Truth of Unhealed Wounds

Through self-discovery and self-healing, I gradually become a conscious parent who is able to connect to my authentic self with less judgment. I get to discover myself and heal more, as I am able to observe and go deeper to reveal my inner child and heal it. During COVID-19, my ten-year-old daughter was doing her home-based learning. She was struggling with attending to schoolwork via an online learning platform. The instructions and deadlines from teachers of different subjects were unclear. She felt discouraged and tried to distract herself by watching YouTube videos every now and then. Whenever I passed by her, she would give me the body language that showed she was shocked, or tried to cover up. After a few times, I decided to speak to her. I told her that if she wished to watch YouTube videos, it would be fine. She just needed to schedule these slots in her timetable so that she would know when to stop and return to her schoolwork. However, I did not like the way she had been dishonest with herself and me. I was unexplainably upset as I expressed my discomfort with her dishonesty. I had not been upset like this for a very long time. I could not calm my mind and kept thinking about how my daughter was hiding something and not able to speak the truth. I had decided to sit with myself and those uncontrollable reactivities and find out what could have been projected within my inner terrain with my daughter's dishonesty. That discomfort was sitting with me for a few days. A few weeks later, I decided to go to a hypnotherapist and intended to work on my inner child's healing.

During the hypnotherapy session, I realized that I was being dishonest when I was around the age of eleven. I could still vividly remember that I was at our primary school dance performance. My dance mates and I were waiting backstage. I was getting ready with my dance costume, and I was panicking because I could not find one of my costume accessories. Shortly, I saw a pair of the costume accessories on a bench. I took the costume accessories away without anyone noticing, and put them on. After that, I saw one of my dance mates and my dance teacher looking for something from a near distance. I did not have the courage to tell them the truth that I took the costume accessories. I was so upset with myself. I could not believe that I did that to my dance mates. I was so dishonest about what happened. Unknowingly, from then onward, I regarded "honesty" as one of the very important values. At that very moment, when I decided not to tell anyone I took the costume accessories, I had paid a big price for not telling the truth. From then on, I have not liked to lie to others. I do not like others to lie to me. Above all, I have lost trust toward myself.

From the session, I got to connect with why it is so important for me to know that my daughter is first being honest with herself and then with others. From that healing session, I became more compassionate with her. She was not yet able to be open to things that she knew she was not able to do—such as she knew she should not play games while doing homework—and she could not openly tell me she wanted to play games. Internally, she might have struggled to admit that she got distracted and decided to play a game. However, she was not ready to take the rejection or "no" from me. She could have feared my reaction after finding out. Therefore, she decided to "hide." Since then, whenever I encounter issues related to honesty, I can choose to stay calm, and not be easily triggered by my old patterns and reactivity from the past. I can listen to others and then accept their choice to tell the truth or not, and I can also invite them to be courageous to tell the truth.

At the end of the day, you are encouraged to accept your children's answer without making them wrong, and encourage them to be courageous and open to face their fear, if any. They can choose not to hide themselves or cover up, as they may need to face natural consequences followed by their choice. No matter what answer they have decided to give you, you know you will be fine and choose not to doubt them.

Barriers between My Child and Me

Over time, as a conscious mother, I have learned about three barriers that get in my way of building strong and close relationships with my child. Once I let go of these three barriers, it has given Ally much space to discover her inner strength and wisdom. Here they are, and I would like to invite you to consider to let go of them to benefit your children's growth too:

1. **Let go of control, so that your children can acquire autonomy.** I have shared a number of examples of how I was a controlling mother. Many times, I realized when I could not let go of control, it was due to my fear, and yes, fear is one of our variety of emotions. Did you notice how frequently you are affected by your mood during the day? If you were to be happy, sad, disappointed, etc., would you allow all these feelings to affect who you are? Unconsciously, you would then allow some of these emotions to control the interaction between you and your child during your precious time together. I can still recall there were a few times I noticed I rushed Ally to speed up finishing her lunch, her homework, her shower, etc., because I did not complete my tasks or work during the day, and I could not be fully present when I was with Ally. This *Disconnected Jenny*, one of my

personalities, robbed away Ally's opportunities to finish her lunch, her homework, her shower...according to her own pace and the quality she might set for herself.

2. **Give up doubt, so that your children find trust in themselves.** There were times where I held tight to my righteousness and said to my Ally that I knew it all. I told her about what successful life meant and she had to follow my advice on her choice of climbing her future career ladder, her choice of picking an ideal future husband, her choice of living her life, her choice of raising a child, etc. based on my own success or failure stories. I did not consider that everyone has their own unique experiences to encounter in life. When I adjust my inner alignment, I know that I need to give up my doubts about whether she would make the *right* choices. I need to give her space to find trust in herself, to unfold her life through experiencing life's ups and downs, to have hope to find strengths, courage, and wisdom in her.

3. **Release fear, so that your children can have the courage to try.** While fear shows up in me as a controlling mother, fear also hides behind me, so that I come across as a "responsible" mother in others' eyes. Before I was a conscious mother, I would sign Ally up at different enrichment classes, so that she could pick up more skills to equip her in the future. When she was

five, I had been wishing for her to take up a musical instrument; she chose violin over piano as she said she could bring the violin around and play. As I was hoping she could do well, I kept telling her that she could do better each time during her practice sessions at home. One day, as I continued to tell her to do better than last practice, she told me, "Mommy, I have been doing my best whenever I practice; I cannot do any better than this, and it is my best right now. I am very tired." Those words woke me up and got me thinking about what I was so anxious for. Gradually, I decided to let her decide her pace.

When Ally was two and a half years old, she told me that she would like to learn ballet. I arranged a trial session for Ally to experience it to see if ballet would be something she enjoyed doing long-term. The feedback from the ballet instructor at that time was that Ally had a hard time following instructions and displaying good self-discipline; hence, she found that Ally was not ready. I told Ally that we would come back to experience ballet dance classes again when she turned three, while I would spend time with her on other alternative activities. We did go back to the ballet dance classes half a year later, and Ally is still dancing ballet to this day. She does at times complain about how much aching she got from dancing, and when I ask her if she would like to stop or continue, she chooses the latter.

Looking back, as I pause and reflect, I can see I was having "the ideal child" in my mind, and I was hoping Ally could dance, play music, draw, paint, etc. Unconsciously I wanted to be seen as a wonderful mother who could raise a well-rounded kid! As my Conscious Parenting journey allows me to get closer to my truth and accept who I am and who I am not, I have become more in tune with who my child is, and I accept that she is not going to be the ideal child I once had in my mind. At the same time, I have also let go of being fearful to be identified as a not-good-enough mother. This has freed Ally up for going along at her pace and being willing to keep trying even when there would be tough times in achieving her own standard of excellence. I do believe that every child wants to do well and every child has unique strengths.

If we look and connect closer with our children, we may notice that our children may also face invisible peer pressure within their social circle. Our children are also wishing they are the one to be praised by teachers, instructors, or someone they look up to before they decide to give up. They are instinctively competitive and want to do better than others too. Our children are afraid of losing out. We as conscious parents can play a part to help our children ease and overcome this fear, to be confident in knowing they have the inner strengths and wisdom to live their life the way they want, and to learn ways to utilize these inner resources.

Would you be able to release your fear, so that your child can gain the courage to try and overcome their own fear?

Conscious Self-Parenting and Reflection

- Let us take a pause here and reflect on whether you have experienced fear whenever you are giving your child opportunities or fear to live their life the way they want. What is this fear all about?
- Put yourself in the shoes of your child. What would he or she gain or lose if you are holding on to these learning opportunities or even mistakes? Would the costs (or losses) outweigh the benefits (gains)?
- What can you do to overcome your own fear?
- What can you do to help your child to overcome his or her fear?

Sometimes, barriers we face may come from our loved ones, not ourselves. In the name of love and care, they give us advice and share their perspectives about the way we parent our children. My mother once told me that I have been using my daughter's future university tuition money on myself by signing up for personal development courses one after another. Here were my self-parenting inner dialogues to get me out from reactivity. I could see my personalities came to play, and how I transformed from shame to compassion:

Misunderstood Jenny felt misjudged by my mother. Her mother's words created much guilt in me. Unconsciously, my automatic reaction went to shame, and I heard my inner self-talk, *I am a bad mother!* followed by, *I should stop spending money on myself!*

Self-Compassionate Jenny took a conscious pause and checked in with herself and said, "This self-parenting journey and these personal growth courses are crucial for Ally and me. Ally gave me a precious moment in my life, and I seized that opportunity, followed by even more learning opportunities, to heal my childhood wounds. I recover my true self by learning from the courses and wisdom teachers. I witness and experience my authentic power, embody, and speak the inner truth. Without the courage to take on those opportunities for self-growth, I would not be who I am today. As I experience love and kindness from within, I want to give love and kindness to Ally and to people around me. Most importantly, I want Ally to witness this possibility of self-transcendence; when she is presented with the options, she can then make her own choices when time comes. Or she can even create other possibilities if she wants to.

Do you not agree? Even with your current way of parenting, you are hoping for the best for your children, so that they are given options and choices to live a better life than ours. How about letting your children define their own "better" life, and we can play the role of empowering them to set up their own options and choices?

Your Child's Ten Essentials

One afternoon, I started a conversation with ten-year-old Ally while we were riding in the car. Ally and I have the habit of asking questions, or sharing what happened during the day, during our car rides. I asked her, "Ally, what are the top ten things in your life that you cannot imagine living without?"

This was how that conversation went:

Me: Number one.

Ally: Roller coasters.

Me: Number two.

Ally: Books.

Me: Number three.

Ally: TV.

Me: Number four.

Ally: Mommy.

Me: Number five.

Ally: Daddy.

Me: Number six.

Ally: Food.

Me: Number seven.

Ally: Ice.

Me: Number eight.

Ally: Milk.

Me: Number nine.

Ally: Candy.

Me: Number ten.

Ally: Onsen.[8]

From the above, I can see the pattern of Ally's thinking process, or even apply it to other children. The first few items that came to her mind would be things that create excitement and allow her to be free to be herself. After that, the listing is followed by things that allow her to feel safe and things that meet her basic needs. Toward the end of the list are things that help her to cope with stress, and things that soothe her or give her pleasure. Of course, the list will change over time. What is more important here is to have many of these conversations for your child to get to know more about themselves. Furthermore, many factors would affect how individuals see the importance of life according to their state of mind: environment (relaxed or stressful), self-talk, upbringing (that can be rooted in the deepest desires), mood, the receiver (who might he/she want to please or had a part to play in the list), etc. Hence, when sharing, it must be the first thing that comes to one's mind, not after deep thinking. Doing this activity is meant to create an opportunity for you to review and practice the five keys to maintain conscious relationships with your child:

1. Mindfully check in with your inner alignment.

8   In Japan, onsen (温泉) are the country's hot springs and the bathing facilities and traditional inns around them.

2. Be a conscious observer of your thinking/feeling/doing.

3. Practice mindful listening to your child or your loved ones in front of you, and listening to your inner voices.

4. Hold space for your authenticity to embrace your emotion at the moment.

5. Insert conscious pause and choose your action or response.

Conscious Self-Parenting and Reflection

- Hold a similar conversation with your children (one at a time, if you have multiple children). Give them your full attention. Ask your child, "(Your child's name), what are the top ten things in your life that you cannot imagine living without?" Ask without judgment and just listen to your child's answers.

- If you like, you can make a list for yourself. Ask yourself, "(Your name), what are the top ten things in your life that you cannot imagine living without?"

- Categorize the above list into (a) things or events that allow you or your child to have freedom to be yourselves; (b) things or events that allow you or your child to be safe or meet the basic needs; and (c) things or events that allow you or your child to cope with stress, or soothe or give pleasure to you, or other categories you may identify along the way.

OUR RELATIONSHIP WITH OUR PARENTS

"How would you describe your relationship with your parents?" This would be one of the questions I asked parents I coached after the first few coaching sessions. While many of my clients would describe conflicts they had with their parents, or pains resulted by unmet needs in their childhood, I did receive a few heartwarming stories that elevated my clients' mood and kept them rooted during challenging times.

"When I was little, whenever I needed to speak to my dad, I would stand in front of him, and he would deliberately put everything away, even the newspaper he read half way, and listen to me intently. I felt respected and important as a child." Daisy continued, "I can still vividly recall this moment, and this precious moment keeps me strong and grounded during difficult times." I could see her eyes brighten up a little. No matter what stories you hang on to up until now, let us use them as our strengths, heal from them, learn from them, and grow from them.

Recall a childhood incident that happened in the past. How did you interpret the experience when you were young? How would your adult self interpret the same incident now? Would you be able to reconcile with what happened in the past? If it is hard to reconcile with this past, and you are still feeling emotional pain, do visit or revisit Chapter 3, and consider suggested ways to heal this childhood wound.

How We Were Parented Affects How We Parent Our Child(ren)

The biggest thing that has benefited me ever since I have become a conscious parent is embracing more self-acceptance and acknowledging that I am whole and complete, even without any acknowledgment from my parents. When I was a child, I longed for my parents' praise and affirmation. I hoped they could see me and hear me, and be proud of who I was when I was doing really well, and praise me for being a "good" girl. The price I paid to be a "good" girl was hiding my true self. I tried to get good grades, to be prefect/monitor in school, to do well in every aspect of my primary school and secondary school, to get recognition and praise, and to say the right things in front of my parents that they would like to hear. However, I could not receive any of those praises, but they would always tell me about someone else's children who were doing so well. If not, they would want me to be a good role model for my younger siblings, or ask me to give in to my siblings, or want me to support my siblings. I felt I was conditionally loved and wondered what about my needs and wants? Who was going to pay attention to me?

Looking back at your childhood, were you considered as a "good" child or the "naughty" one by your parents? If you were labeled, how did it make you feel? How does it affect the way you behave or make decisions as an adult later in life?

Conscious Self-Parenting and Reflection

Have you ever labeled your child as "good," "naughty," "disobedient," etc.? What do you think your child would feel after being labeled? Please pay attention to your child's behaviors as he or she is labeled, and make a conscious choice whether you are going to do something differently?

Again, I paid a price to be a good girl to get my parents' affirmation: I started disliking the incongruent me. Inside of me, I felt I was not good enough, that I did not deserve love. I felt awfully bad about how I could not live up to my parents' expectation to be a successful person who earned lots of money, drove a big car, stayed in a bungalow, and needed not worry about money when I was a young adult. Their yardstick of success is nothing about honoring them or me, but predetermined by people around us and the society we are living in. Outside of me, I was unconsciously wanting to look good in front of others. I cared about what others thought of me. I could not have the freedom to be me. I said things that others wanted to hear. I did things so that I could get recognition. I seemed to be in a mess. I was operating from a place of fear as a new parent.

Can I do this the right way? What if I cannot be a good enough mother?

I could still remember, in the labor room, I felt empty when I saw my baby at first sight. I did not know what to feel. My heart was murmuring, *What is wrong with me? Why am I not feeling anything? Should I not be happy to see my baby?* I could only make sense out of this after I became a conscious mother. My fear of not being able to be a good enough mother blocked me from feeling joy. Although I did not go into any depression or postnatal blues, I was struggling to cope with my physical and emotional needs. Not until that night—the magical touch that my daughter gave me when she was two months old—did I shift from numbness to a sense of unconditional love. Her index finger touched my cheek; I interpreted it as a touch of unconditional love. This touch helped me to realize I needed to first accept myself. If my daughter could fully and unconditionally accept me for who I was and was not, who I am and am not, and who I will be and will not be, why could I not honor and accept myself?

Since I have set off on the Conscious Parenting journey, I am able to become more aware of myself and my thoughts. As an observer of my life, I can detach from my meaning-making mind, and everything becomes simpler and clearer. My cluttered and noisy voices in my mind became quieter. I was able to be fully present with my daughter and her needs. I could see the differences of my parenting styles before and after becoming a conscious parent.

Before I became a conscious parent	After I became a conscious parent
I was the director of my child's play; my child was required to follow my instructions.	I am an observer of my child's play; I see her strengths and personal traits while spending time with her.
I was overly sensitive about how others viewed me.	I can accept myself for who I am and who I am not. At the same time, I hold space for myself and others, should they share their views of me.
I frequently felt regret for what I did or did not do, and I hated that regret.	Because I can remind myself to live in the present moment, I make better choices without fear or regret.
I used to be full of self-doubt and held unlimited judgment against myself.	I can embrace my mistakes and take them as learning opportunities. I can laugh at myself and feel compassionate toward myself.

"I Cannot Feel Your Love!"

Since the 18th of March 2020, the Singapore government imposed additional border controls and travel restrictions due to the COVID-19 pandemic and I had not been able to visit my parents who live in Johor Bahru, Malaysia. Restrictions on movements between Singapore and Malaysia were announced to tackle the spread of the coronavirus, and some 300,000 people were affected as they moved across the land crossings on a daily basis for work or study or leisure.[9] My husband, daughter,

9   Su, "Bags Packed, Malaysians Stream into Singapore."

and I used to go back every other weekend to visit my parents and spend quality time together. Since restrictions on movement announcements between the two countries, we have been using videoconferencing to speak to one another at least once a week. My mother and my siblings join me at Wu Tao Dance online sessions weekly, and we catch up after the end of the dance session. I speak to my father once or twice a month; he is not used to phone calls or online video conferences. In August 2021, during his birthday celebration, we had a video conferencing session. He was in a good mood to chat with us more. As he was slightly more chatty than usual, I gathered that he probably had some drinks before the call.

Here is our conversation, translated from Mandarin Chinese:

My dad: You are too stubborn. You never express yourself
    clearly with the person you have an issue with.
Me: Dad, I do not understand what you are referring to. Can
    you give me a specific example?
He looks away.
Me: Dad, do you know things I say and do are all out of a
    place of love?
My dad: Love? I cannot feel your love.

Then and there, I was a little stunned to hear that. I did not know what to say. I felt my heart was soaked in bitterness; after all, my father still did not understand me, or he misunderstood me. I was uncontrollably sad the following few days. My heart was as heavy as a rock and kept sinking. I carried this rock everywhere I went, at work and at home. Why was this trigger so clingy this time? I was holding a compassionate space for this state of mine. One morning, after my meditation, I was journaling about the heaviness in me, and I found out that I had expectations of my father. "My dad should understand everything I do, and he should love me for who I am and who I am not."

All these shoulds and my expectations of him had kidnapped me and my self-love. I was looking for love from outside. I felt I fell into the trap of lack again. I had gotten on healing my wounded inner child since 2016, layer by layer. I shed so many layers that got my true self hidden deep inside. At that moment, I realized that I still had the need for my father's trust and love. The little Jenny who needed her father's trust showed up. The *Misunderstood Jenny* (Chapter 3) who did not want to be misunderstood was called out. I meditated and connected with my inner wounds. I decided to accept myself for who I am and what I do, accept and face what my father said and did not say. This acceptance had opened up a space for my heart to beat freely without feeling the heaviness in it again.

After that, I called my dad again and told him how grateful I was that he gave me every opportunity he could, so that I have the ability to earn a living and sustain my livelihood. He sponsored my degree to study in the United States. I was a graduate with a bachelor of science in management information systems. I found a job as a content engineer developing Singapore's first Chinese search engine through this degree. I moved to Singapore, settled down, married, and had a child because of that stepping stone.

To be an awakened and conscious being has allowed me to bounce back quicker and quicker without being a whiny little child who felt misunderstood and "abandoned" once more. Every time the bounce back has made me wiser and more courageous to transform my pains, and I am grateful to my inner self who once yearned for help and whispered to me and told me, *Let me out of this dark and suffocating dungeon!* I get to see my courageous true self.

Conscious Self-Parenting and Reflection

Have you ever noticed that you or someone you know has spiraled into a habitual pattern or an old pain again and again? If yes, how did you or the person manage to break the chain of pattern or pain (see Chapter 3)? Or are you or the  person still being spiraled into or stuck in this old habitual cycle? I am inviting you to apply the techniques and methods to unchain yourself from this old habitual cycle.

MY RELATIONSHIP WITH MY SPOUSE

I once caught my wounded inner child in the "mirror" my husband projected and shone back to me.

I had not completely accepted myself.

I have been practicing meditation since 2016. I would describe myself as a good observer and I am able to regulate my emotions a lot better as compared to not practicing it in the years before 2016. It is now integrated into my daily morning routine as a part of showing myself the importance of self-love. I am able to watch my emotion coming and decide if I could hold a space for it or do something about it. I am fully aware of being responsible for my own emotions. I am fully aware of being responsible for my own emotions, and I can recognize when an emotion is not tied to the present but rather a past memory.

One morning my husband kissed me goodbye and said, "I love you" before he went off to work. Immediately, I could sense *I-Do-Not-Need-It Jenny* show up, and I behaved like I could not care more from the outside. Deep inside, I heard my inner voice say, *Why have I not felt much when I received his words "I love you" lately? I wonder if there is a part of me that I have yet to fully accept myself, and I feel lacking somewhere.*

Of course, there could be a variety of interpretations of why I could not feel much. I could give excuses all I wanted:

- *We have been married for nineteen years; it has been so long that we have lost the passion!* And I would do nothing about it.
- *We have some conflicts here and there after all these years. I have gathered that he "only cares about himself."* It is hard for him to understand my point of view. In this case, I

would make myself a victim and hope he could come around one day, and again, I would do nothing about it.

However, I realized *there is a part of me that I have yet to fully accept myself*. I became curious about where I needed to heal. I got to take the power back to myself, and decided to do something about it. Later on, I took time to meditate and did journaling, so that I could have a conversation with myself about possible triggers or areas where I had yet to accept myself fully. By now, I was familiar with the work of self-acceptance; it would take time to discover different emotional reactions after the trigger went off. This time, I felt numbed about the expression of "I love you." I felt the avoidance of trusting love (from my husband, or in fact, at a deeper level from myself), which was similar to my blind spot—*I do not deserve love*.

During meditation around this time, I felt pain near my heart area. In my mind, there was an image of me. I was trying to reach out to someone. I felt like a very young child, I might have been a toddler then, and my heart was whispering, "Do not go." As I was asking my mother, she said there was a time when I was around a year old, and my father and my mother had to attend to their businesses and left me with my grandmother for a few weeks in a rural area. It was about a three- to four-hour drive away from where my parents stayed. After hearing what my mother said, I connected this as my interpretation of abandonment; it was how I felt at that time. This could be where it all started; it could be the origin of my blind spot and interpretation of my parents' love for me. *I do not deserve love.* I felt pain in my chest, and I could not understand why I was left behind, and I shed tears during my meditation session.

The above was another level of discovery of why that disconnection was within me. As I expressed this disconnection this time around, I felt numb and empty. Strangely, for some reasons, I did not feel sad, but I could talk about it with a smile and stay calm. I might have taken off my "armor," the way I chose to protect myself, and how I wanted people to "see" me. When I had not been getting in touch with my deeper emotion, this belief and pain of *I do not deserve love* would surface out in another form. I would look inside myself, meditate, and do journaling, and be curiously interested in which part of myself would need some healing this time.

Because I am able to apply conscious pauses, I can see how my past wants to infiltrate the present moment, and I can then disrupt my own patterns by putting a "brake" in my thinking and doing. After that, I would choose to see and hear the person whom I was interacting with, and hold honor for who he or she is, rather than projecting the ideal person I wish to see. I am totally aware that there is no perfection or no destination in maintaining relationships with others; it is only in the present moment, the here and now that is more important than the past and the future. I am in charge of my inner weather; I am able to provide a safe space that is nonjudgmental for my loved ones by observing moment-by-moment shifting and the cause and effect of my responses.

As we practice mindfulness, we are able to pay attention to and take care of our inner terrain and inner weather. Watching inner weather can be further elaborated like watching your thoughts and emotions is like watching the floating cloud in the sky when staying in the present moment. You know and are aware of your thoughts and emotions that come and go. Unlike your old being or unconscious mind, you may have been brought to the past, you feel guilty about what you did not do or could have done, or cling on to how you were happier then, etc. Staying in the past will block you from staying in the present moment and enjoying what you have in the here and now. Furthermore, holding on to the past may also stir up painful emotions. There is nothing wrong in planning for the future, as it brings you hope, aspiration, and vision to move toward your goals, as long as you stay rooted and curious to face the uncertainties in the future. Be courageous and positive to tell yourself that you got this. Or else, you might be spiraled into the worrying tornado. Having been aware of how your mind time-travels, where would you like to be? The past, present, or future? Would you be able to bring yourself back to the present consistently to exercise your power of present?

Through my self-parenting and healing journey, I am continuously strengthening the unity and connection of my body, mind, and soul. With this inner alignment, I know why I choose to be a Conscious Parenting coach, as it aligns with my value, which is the kind of growing-up space I wish I have. I hope children can grow up to connect with their inner truth and access their inner resources that give them strength and courage to live their life, not to live their parents' delusion of their life. I have grown so much in self-awareness and become less self-centered like the world only revolves around me. I can stay grounded where I am and be who I am. I get to experience aliveness at a deeper level; it is no longer about achieving life goals how others and the society define them. As a result of honoring my being through ever-evolving self-growth, it emanates love and kindness; this being simply contributes to others without forceful action.

Past......   Present   ......Future

Inner Weather: Mind Time-Travel into the Present? The Past? Or the Future?

Conscious Self-Parenting and Reflection

Having sorted it out within me, I also invited my husband to do this exercise. To sit face-to-face for three minutes, and literally to see each other eye to eye. You are welcome to try this out.

- Make eye contact at the same level, using a soft gaze.
- Decide one to lead and the other to follow. Say aloud one sentence at a time. The other repeats after the lead. You may say your favorite phrases or create your own. The intention is to support and remind each other of this lifetime partnership. Some ideas of phrases:
  - Thích Nhất Hạnh's mantras; see also "My go-to wisdom teachers" section:
    - *"Darling, I am here for you."*
    - *"Darling, I know you are there."*
- Repeat three times.

At this point you may ask, *What if my spouse is not interested in learning more or becoming a conscious parent? What is the point if I am a conscious parent? We are supposed to work as a team to raise our children, are we not?* Our aim here is not to force anyone into a new way of parenting, or even being, when he or she is not ready. However, when we experience it ourselves and benefit from it, we can share it as a possibility for our spouse, or even our friends, to consider and take the first step. Here is what I will tell you and answer the above questions, which I have learned from my spouse after all these years:

You cannot change the past; however, you can choose to heal from it. From the process of healing, you can find peace and love. When you are ready, you will need the courage to face your emotional pain. This time around you are not alone, as

I am here to walk this path together with you. This is a life-long journey. I know it for sure that this growth makes us humans beautiful. It is okay if you are not ready. This is your life, and it requires you to decide whether you want to take up your life's work. No one else should tell you what to do, but to show you the possibilities. Hence, I shall learn how to accept and respect your choice. Just like our children. They accept who we are as their parents; they show us the possibilities to outgrow our inner child. You and I receive that gift from our children. We are learning to be better parents, in fact, to reveal our true selves. Our children are there with us as we walk the path. This makes our parent–child relationships and growing path so beautiful. Once again, my heart is wide open; I am practicing to be as present and mindful as I can. I will be here always to attend to your questions. In fact, you are holding me to be accountable for putting conscious self-parenting and parenting in action day by day.

Yes, you and I need to take the first step first, before we find another "reason" to stop ourselves from taking action.

five

LIFE IS ABOUT TAKING ACCOUNTABILITY

"How is life?" I can still remember when I first went to the United States and pursued my bachelor's degree at the age of nineteen. I worked at the university's cafeteria as a cashier. Once, one of the patrons was making payment for a coffee while striking a conversation and asked me, "How is life?" I actually went into a deep thought. I was running through my thoughts, and trying to feel and summarize my life, and wanting to give a genuine answer. As people waiting in line at my counter were getting crowded, I was startled and came back to myself, and quickly replied, "Good," and moved on. How many times in life do we just let our busy schedules push us forward, and when you do have time to pause and look back, how much regret and guilt have we been repeatedly wanting to stop?

How many of us will intentionally insert a pause, decide to turn things around, and tell ourselves, *I have enough regrets and guilt! I am going to take charge of my life!* How many of us can own up to the decision made, and be responsible and be courageous to face whatever consequences resulted from the decisions we made? At times, you need to even own up to the decisions you did not make and be aware that *even if you do not make any decisions*, it is still a choice of not making any decisions. How many of us have fallen into a cycle of bad choices, and we are still making the same decision that did not work, still sticking to the miseries over and over again?

When I was working as a parenting program manager, one of my superiors recommended a book to me. I was reading it as part of my research on choice and decision-making. I saw this paragraph, and it aligned with what I am describing here. It serves as supporting evidence.

What my superior and I spoke about Choice Theory could be the origin of why I decided to bring this paragraph in.

Children's upbringing is highly influenced by parents and decisions they made. More than usual, parents are making these decisions unconsciously thinking they are for the best of their children's sake. However, if we take a deeper look, these decisions were indirectly caused by their childhood wounds they wanted to avoid, or happy moments they wanted to keep.

For instance, sending my daughter to local public school was a decision my husband made, and a decision I did not object to when she turned five years old. Before the decision was made, there were three key criteria set for the school chosen: educational programs and frameworks, distance from home, and affordability. When my husband commented that the nearby government school he picked met all of the key criteria, I was a little reluctant to agree on the school's educational program and framework, because it was too similar to my primary school back in my hometown (i.e., strict traditional Chinese education, traditional instruction and teacher-centric model, when I would prefer a learner-centric model). I was aware of why I was hesitating: I hope Ally will grow up to stand on her own feet and think for herself. She will retain her natural curiosity to discern how things work and how they may affect her life and work in the short and long run. Yes, this was also related to my growing up, and skills that I hoped I could pick up at a younger age. Furthermore, I was hoping she would have a smoother transition from a relatively authentic Montessori nursery and kindergarten to primary school. Since the nearby government school my husband picked was something that worked better operationally for the entire six years, I did not object and go along, and even joined forces with my husband to clock in the required eighty hours as parent volunteers, so that we could meet the minimum enrollment requirements.

Today, Ally is graduating from this nearby government school, and she has also completed her national examination where her results will decide whether she gets to enter the secondary school(s) she applies for. Looking back, for the six years she attended that school, there were ups and downs during her learning journey; she went through struggles and pains to understand some hard truths and rejections, especially during the COVID-19 period. Generally, all three of us did our best in getting through this journey. Although these were unforeseeable circumstances, I had to be accountable for the decision I did not object to, and learned along the way about myself and with her. As a conscious mother, I know I have multiple roles to play in bridging her past experiences, and together with Ally, we will also strengthen our resilience and stay rooted in allowing things to unfold along this upcoming learning journey. Of course, we are continuously connecting our lives in the present moment. The hard truths and rejections she encountered during primary school have reflected the reality she may be facing in the real world; however, at times, it was painful for me to watch and support her at the side:

- *Loads of homework from multiple subjects on the same day was a way of learning.* While I could help her to acknowledge the intention of teachers and homework design the way it was, this was contrasting to what she believed in. To her, tests and assignments to be given and completed in school would be more efficient and effective for her to learn.

- *One-way respect to authority figures.* Yes, as a student, she learned that she would have to accept everything teachers said unconditionally, even though these messages might be unconsciously shaming the students. From her point of view, when students' voices were heard, even if the voices were to explain why they did not submit their homework, students would be open to reflect what they could do differently and increase their will to take on the accountability.

- *Enthusiasm in learners was meaningless.* The hard truth she learned was even if you would be enthusiastic to learn and contribute through raising your hand up high to ask or answer questions, it would not be recognized and opportunities might not be given to you.

Parents, we ought to show up for our children, help them bridge family values and cultural conditioning, understand the world we are living in, and be accountable for the decisions we make for ourselves and our children. As our children are walking alongside us, they gradually pick up decision-making skills. For instance, first, to have an inquiring mind able to lay out all their options; second, to align and weigh their options with the decision criteria; and lastly, to own their final decision and be ready to face any consequences. The more clarity we have in our decision-making process, the more prepared we are for the consequences. In order to have clarity, we are first required to have clarity within our being.

Conscious Self-Parenting and Reflection

- As a parent, are you able to show up for your child(ren) every single time to go through the ups and downs with him or her?
- Were there times you were running away or hiding from being accountable for the consequences of decisions made? What would be some reason(s) for you running away? Were you afraid of losing something (e.g., a thing, a relationship, your pride and your protection layer or ego) (e.g., to admit or face your weakness)? Did you lose something, or was it just your imagined loss? What did you learn from there?

Let us take a closer look at how our being (i.e., our thoughts, feelings, and actions) affects our decision-making.

According to William Glasser's *Choice Theory*,

...for all practical purposes, we choose *everything* we do, including the misery we feel. Other people can neither make us miserable nor make us happy. All we can get from them or give to them is information. But by itself, information cannot make us do or feel anything. It goes into our brains, where we process it and then decide what to do... As bad as you may feel, much of what goes on in your body when you are in pain or sick is the indirect result of the actions and thoughts you choose or have chosen every day of your life.[1]

Being a critical thinking educator for many years, I always bring this awareness to students that what they think, feel, and do is highly interconnected. As soon as one consciously decides their thoughts for the day, it is going to affect how they feel and what they do, and the results of the action. For instance, when students have a preconception or stereotype about Monday after a weekend break from school. On Monday morning, their mind may fill with "I am having Monday blues." They may feel down, experience negative feelings, and then drag their body to school. Throughout the day, until they are able to make a conscious choice to reframe their thought or realign themselves with their values-based action (e.g., "I value collaborative learning and I know there is something I can offer to my peer discussion" or "No one cares to listen to what I have to say. I do not belong here," etc.), they may gain or miss some good learning opportunities with their peers for the day."

---

1   Glasser, *Choice Theory*, 3–4.

Later on, I discovered that this aligns with cognitive behavioral theory (CBT). Hence, consciously making the right choice for that present moment will help how things such as parent–child interactions turn out. To further elaborate my point on the importance of a conscious choice, apart from Dr. William Glasser's *Choice Theory*, Dr. John Calvin Chatlos's awareness of the experience of "being" as he described in his article,

> Often, people believe and act as if they "are" what they feel, or "are" what they think, rather than realizing that feelings and thoughts occur automatically until conscious choice occurs. Conscious awareness of our human ability to "choose" our response to our feelings, thoughts and urges to act is necessary for the transition from the outside objective world into the awareness of "being"...[2]

Hence, to have the ability to evaluate data received through five senses and make informed decisions, one can pick a different start point that will lead you to a different end point. In other words, as a conscious observer, having zoomed into our moment-by-moment observation of experience, we can be more aware of the information or data we receive—through our body that receives sensory information, thoughts, and feelings that may occur automatically in the background until we make a choice to respond and act accordingly. However, when we have

---

2   Chatlos, "Framework of Spirituality," 311.

yet to practice and apply mindfulness and become a conscious observer, we may follow our habitual patterns or unconsciously allow automatic reactions to take place. It is important for us to be aware of how we can take the power back by being a responsible adult and paying attention to our decision-making process.

Your Attitudes Drive Your Life. Adapted from Figure 1 in Chatlos, "Framework of Spirituality," 311.

Through your basic senses, you can interpret outside information and decide internally what to do next. Your body uses five senses to collect information and affect your thinking and doing, which affects the way you feel; therefore, it affects your being. For example, a mom sees her child sitting in front of a computer. Her expectation and prior beliefs help her interpret what she sees in the present moment, which is based on similar past experiences, and a thought arises unconsciously, *My child is playing online games again!* She feels warmth in her cheeks, a clenched jaw, and an inner voice follows: *I am very upset! I told her not to...* Her habitual pattern reacting to this particular behavior of her child is to yell at her child first. Because Mom values time spent well, the next thing she does is to remove her computer. The consequence is the child yells back and tries very hard to take back the computer. Mom's attitude toward her child sitting in front of a computer is worrying. She is worried her child might have an online game addiction. In other words, Mom's attitude toward her child is fueled by a potential addiction to online games and influences her choice of action and responses to her perceived challenge in getting her child to stop sitting in front of a computer. This mom might be hijacked by her anxious emotion and react directly, until she realizes she can make a conscious choice to choose her thought or action (i.e., she can be curious and open-minded to check with her child to find out what her child is doing when she sees her child sitting in front of a computer).

Additionally, we interpret information based on our beliefs, values, judgment, biases, and expectations. Due to stress level and coping strategies available at the moment, our thoughts then make decisions and take actions from there.

As a conscious parent, knowing your choices and options and being aware of the consequences of your selected choice are important, especially when you are judging your child's behavior from the surface and unable to see the underlying emotions beyond your child's behavior. Here is an example of my daily interaction with my daughter: Ally came to me and wanted me to listen to her while I was folding clothes. I was exhausted after a long day with a demanding schedule; however, I tried to make myself available for my daughter, as I treasured my time with her. Every sentence she said, I was proactively participating, and responding to my twelve-year-old daughter.

Ally: Mommy, you are not listening to me.

Me: I am listening to you attentively; that is why I am responding to everything you say.

Ally: Can you just listen to me?

Me: Okay. (I keep my mouth shut tightly and stay quiet with an unreluctant and resisting energy as I feel rejected by her with my proactive participation in the conversation.)

Ally (says what she says, waits for me to reply): Mommy, did you hear me? Why are you not saying anything?

Me (getting myself triggered and reacting immediately after listening to what she has said): What do you want Mommy to do and say? When I replied earlier, you said

I did not hear you. Now when I do not say anything, you
blame Mommy for not responding to you!
Tears roll down Ally's cheeks, and she walks away.

Having practiced mindfulness for many years now, you may
think that I would be more aware of thoughts and emotions.
During the above interaction, I learned from Ally that I was not
connected with my other emotions well, such as emotional
numbness or feeling numb. At that moment, I was present to
my external experience with openness and nonjudgment (e.g.,
what happened and what Ally said). However, I did not pay full
attention to my internal experience (e.g., my physical exhaustion, my feeling of tiredness, and my blank mind). Most importantly, I did not consciously connect with my inner alignment
in terms of acknowledging my numbing thinking and feeling. Hence, I did not have the space or "freedom" to choose
and take values-based action. I am not finding an excuse and
saying I was exhausted at that moment. Having reflected on
what happened, if I could own my side-by-side emotions such
as exhaustion (body and mind worn out) and enthusiasm (listening to her) and allow myself to share with her my state and
internal experience, acknowledging I might not be able to
fully present, it could help us to hold the space for each other
compassionately.

I realize that the bare awareness is not enough, and the
qualities of our attention paid moment-to-moment counts.
Connecting back to Shapiro et al., the attitude we bring to

the attention is essential.[3] To better recognize our attitude and inner alignment, we can observe the integration of our thoughts, feelings, and actions.[4] To be able to take values-based action, mindfulness can help us to minimize distraction, avoid judgmental thoughts, or be more attuned with our numbing thoughts and feelings. This "open, intentional awareness can help us choose behaviors that are congruent with our needs, interests and values."[5] The ability to make space to pause and respond with greater freedom of choice (i.e., in less conditioned, automatic ways) helps us make a more conscious and informed choice of action.

HOLDING SPACE FOR MY CLIENT

At work, Jessica found out that she was being demoted. On one hand, she felt betrayed by her company where she worked really hard for the past decade; on the other hand, she felt so much guilt for spending much less time as she wished to with her children. She believed that she sacrificed a lot of her family time for her work, and yet, demotion was the answer to her hard work and sacrifices. She felt tremendous stress, and she was not ready to cope with this unexpected news from work.

---

3   Shapiro et al., "Mechanisms of Mindfulness."
4   Chatlos, "Framework of Spirituality."
5   Shapiro et al., "Mechanisms of Mindfulness."

Jessica teared up during our online coaching session. She cried, "I want to run away. I want to go somewhere very, very far away. I want to escape from where I am now. I am trapped."

Listening to Jessica at the session, I could see clearly how I was in the fight-or-flight mode, dealing with emotional traps, back in 2007. I could feel how Jessica felt at the moment: heavy-hearted, suffocated in a vacuum, unable to see things clearly, mourning her unfair life.

I was no stranger to this resisting voice, this belief that "My freedom was robbed."

I asked Jessica if she had accepted what happened, and if she was ready to move on.

"I am not sure," she said.

Although we generally know that the only person whose behavior we can control or change is ourself, we cannot help to always want to change others; if not, we find ourselves as a victim of a situation. Jessica chose to believe that she was a victim of the demotion situation. "No matter how hard I tried in the past decade, this was the answer to my devotion at work," she repeated. At this point, due to the self-limiting beliefs, she had spiraled into a state of disappointment; she felt betrayed. This created a psychological barrier that might have blocked her openness in possibly reframing the way she could see this differently. The more she saw herself as a victim, the more reluctant she would be to explore other alternative options, and hence, she got stuck. According to Glasser, "All behavior is total behavior and is made up of four inseparable components: acting, thinking, feeling and physiology... All total behavior is chosen, but we have direct control over only the acting and thinking components."[6] In Jessica's case, due to the negative thinking she had unconsciously chosen, it created a downward spiral and stress for her at work and at home. This sense of helplessness was a result of her thoughts, where this thought might have been seen by Jessica as reality. The truth was it was just a thought she could decide to cling onto, replace with alternative thought, or let go of. In fact, at a deeper level, a wounded inner child in Jessica was repressing the betrayal she once experienced in the past. This was also the habitual pattern she repeated when confronted by the pain from betrayal. Until she was able to put a stop to this habitual pattern, which consistently brought her back to the pain of feeling betrayal, by shifting her thinking, perceived pain would be the portal of her transformation.

It is also human nature that we make choices to avoid or decrease pain or make choices that create or increase pleasure. This is the core of how we make decisions, which is suggested by Sigmund Freud, which is also known as the pain pleasure principle. As our beliefs, values, actions, and decisions are built upon this principle and how we interpret the situation in front of us, much is affected by our beliefs and values, based on our personal past experiences. We seek pleasure to reward ourselves with immediate gratification. We seek instant gratification and

6   Glasser, *Choice Theory*, 336.

avoid pain. When we face conflict, we interpret it as painful and will do anything to avoid conflict. What is even more painful for us is the thought of dealing with this conflict, facing our pain, or even at some point, having to admit that we have a part to play in creating conflict. How painful when we have to admit that we have a part to play in the conflict, which also means that we are not good enough to manage conflict or avoid conflict! How dumb for not being "smart" enough to handle potential negative situations in the first place! Deep down, *I am not good enough!* may surface, which is another thing we are trying to avoid, and yes, I am not any smarter than you to avoid this conflict. Ouch! It is painful to have the other party to see that *I am not smarter than you!* It is painful to realize that *I am not good enough!* When we miss the opportunity to take on self-acceptance and our imperfection, this thinking trap of *I am not good enough* will create furious resistance in us when someone is trying to persuade us to face our pain, or to get help from others.

Alternatively, what if Jessica chose to see this demotion situation as an opportunity to grow and get to know more about herself? At the beginning of this chapter, we know that a different thought and/or a different action would bring a different outcome. What if Jessica could pause and also check in with her feelings and physiological responses first, and then choose her thoughts and/or actions? She would pause and notice information sent through her senses and body. For example, she first had a thought that she was demoted due to an unappreciative new boss. As she was observing that thought, giving herself a pause, and her mind/thoughts quieted down, she noticed her body sensation and heard this from within: *I am feeling sad, and I am sensing a tight chest in my body right now; I wonder, where is this coming from? Let me give some space for this tight chest and accept it at this moment. It is okay to feel this way right now.* She might have slight relief from the constriction in her chest as she was acknowledging it. When she was able to regulate her emotion, she freed up space to think about some options to face this situation:

- Speak to her superior and understand what she could do to build a productive relationship with her superior. She could potentially discuss the values she could bring to the table and to their team, and negotiate for a period of learning and growth for both ends; or
- Choose to take this as an opportunity to spend quality time with her children while exploring her next move; or
- Be curious about what she would need to learn from this situation, and acknowledge how she could be emotionally hijacked by her wounded inner child, and consider how to heal her inner wound; or
- Give herself time to sit side-by-side with this feeling and get to know this personality before she could proceed to her next step; and more.

As a Conscious Parenting coach, I would feel what Jessica felt, and coregulate with her. To stay with her like the cotton tree (see Chapter 3) and hold space for her to feel safe to face her vulnerability, to allow her to sense and feel the emotion in her body, so that she could observe the effects of hanging on to this state. She could then pause gently, access her inner resources, and make a conscious choice of her action when she was ready.

Conscious Self-Parenting and Reflection

Let us be curious about what you would do if you were Jessica. Or, bring in your own difficult situation and reflect. You could first check in with yourself by journaling and using these questions as prompts:

- What could I learn from this unforeseen circumstance?
- Could I reframe my demotion/difficult situation from something bad that happened to me to something good? (For example, Jessica wanted to be more involved in her children's lives, and this demotion enabled her to do that.)
- Where do I want to lead my life and my family from here on?
- How can I tap into my strengths to manage this challenging time?

As you are reperceiving or reframing your situation that may make a shift of your perspective, you may notice some emotion and body sensation arise. You may close your eyes and be present to your emotion and body sensation with openness, no judgment, and compassion. Sit with that state and allow space to hold that emotion until you are ready to open your eyes. You may pen down or draw your inner experience.

As she was taking time to get clarity from within, she was able to shift her perspective from a *victim mentality to the author of her life*, and she started making some responsible choices. I could encourage Jessica to deconstruct her attitude toward life and look into her thinking, feeling and, doing (behavior) by following the "Observing Self (Stage 1)" structure.

OBSERVING SELF (STAGE 1)

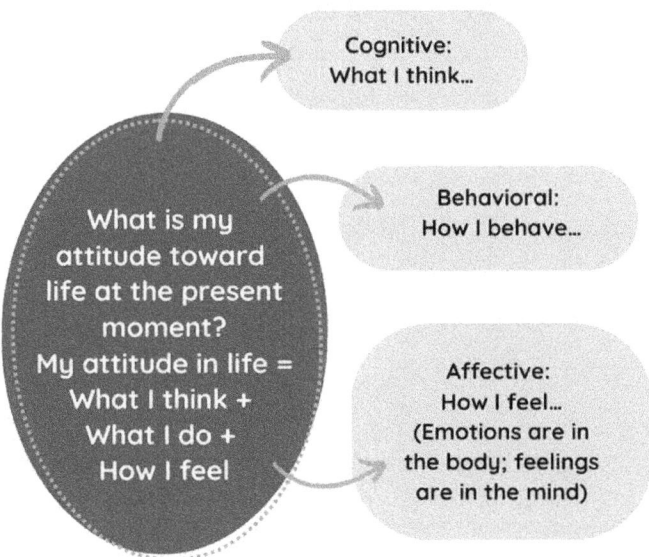

What is my attitude toward life at the present moment?
My attitude in life =
What I think +
What I do +
How I feel

Cognitive:
What I think...

Behavioral:
How I behave...

Affective:
How I feel...
(Emotions are in the body; feelings are in the mind)

Observing Self (Stage I)

What is my attitude toward life at the present moment?

My attitude in life = What I think + What I do + How I feel

Cognitive. What I think...

I view myself as a committed employee. Recently, my company demoted me, despite my more than a decade of commitment and service. I have no say in what happens to me.

Behavioral. How I behave...

I avoid talking to my new superior and colleagues, whom I have worked with for so many years. I regret sacrificing my family time for a company that did not appreciate me. I am now sick and tired of my job here. I am a victim in this incident, and there is nothing much I can do.

Affective. How I feel... (Emotions are in the body; feelings are in the mind)

I feel betrayed. I feel pain.

How might things have changed if the initial thought had not been *I have no say in what happens to me?* What if instead, Jessica's thought had been, *I do not think I deserve this demotion.*

I am curious about how this decision was made. I need to talk to HR personnel. In a larger picture, Jessica's attitude toward life is I have no say in what happens to me, and this attitude follows her in many areas of her life, such as dealing with working relationships and couple relationships. Whenever an authoritarian figure gets in her way, she may be triggered and perceive herself as the powerless one. How might this have shown up in her parent–child relationships? When she faced self-help-lessness in front of her children and unconsciously thought, *I have no say in what happens to me*, she might have chosen to run away from the situation, or to be hijacked by her emotions and could not calmly access her inner resources. To build closer parent–child relationships, Jessica can choose to practice and integrate mindfulness in her daily routine, apply the four-step CARE Method, and put a stop to her pain by embarking on her wounded inner child healing journey.

Conscious Self-Parenting and Reflection

When you find yourself stuck, you may take time and deconstruct your thinking, feeling, and behavior using the following structure:

- How do you know when you are stuck?
- When do you become self-centered, like the earth only revolves around you?
- How do you usually get unstuck?

As you are reflecting and filling up the table at below, think of each table column like a drawer, be curiously interested in "pulling out each drawer" one at a time, and finding out what they are inside your *think, behave (do)*, and *feel* drawers.

Observing Self (Stage I)

What is my attitude toward life at the present moment?	What I think...	How I behave...	How I feel...
My attitude in life = What I think + What I do + How I feel			

Before we can make any conscious choices, we need to be aware of what is happening inside us, such as our thinking and feeling, toward this conscious decision-making process? Through the process, we will be able to get clarity of why this decision-making process is needed/required, and whether each of these choices may drive us toward betterment in life, or if they are just some impulsive decision because we are resisting or avoiding ourselves or others.

We can check in with ourselves and ask these questions.

HOW DOES MY BODY FEEL?

First of all, you can feel the shift in your physiological state, e.g., rapid heart beats, warm cheeks, tight chest, tight jaws, etc.

You may consider making a pros and cons list about the options you have before making a decision on which one of the options you would like to move forward. As you go through each option in the list, you can scan your body and check its sensations given on each option:

- Does it give you an expansion where your heart feels full?
- Does it give you a contraction where you feel tightness in your chest?
- Do you have butterflies in your stomach?
- Do you feel excited or get inspired with goose bumps?

Your body is giving you information, receiving it through deep listening to your heart's whisper.

IS THIS FAMILIAR?

We need to be aware of our old patterns when it comes to decision-making. One of the old patterns or habits may be making decisions impulsively when our thought process is blinded by our feelings. In other words, we make decisions based on how we feel. For example, when we feel sad, we crave and buy ice cream to cheer ourselves up. Or, we change our job because our boss makes us feel lousy after we work so hard.

We must not make decisions when we are emotional. We can choose to calm ourselves down first, acknowledge and reflect on what may be blinding us at the present moment, and potentially lead you away from making impulsive decisions that you may regret later on, which might not be your first time making such impulsive decisions driven by your emotions.

IS THERE ANYTHING I NEED TO LEARN AT THIS MOMENT?

Be responsible and bold to tell yourself that you are in charge of this internal conversation, you have options, and you can decide how to respond in this instance, and move forward. For example, "I can pay attention to what my child is trying to tell me through her behavior; does she need my help?" Before I respond, I clarify my interpretation and communicate out of love or in service to the other party. If I am experiencing fear, I can choose to detach from my emotions and simply notice that I am trying to "win over the battle" and there is no battle to win in the first place but love.

HOW CAN I COMMUNICATE WITH CLARITY?

As long as you choose to move away from the emotional baggage and do something, you will have the space to communicate with the other party even if you need to hold the space for both you and her to agree with the disagreement. Use *I* statements, and notice if you are using "I think" or "I feel." These statements indicate you are ready to own your feelings, thinking, concerns, and needs without blaming others or sounding defensive. The source of your judgmental mind usually comes from survival mode. These reactive and judgmental thoughts could be coming from survival mode, which is usually trying to control the other party because of your internal insecurity. You can then choose to pause, and choose again. In contrast, the gut is intuitive, sending implicit messages about our deeper needs and offering very little explanation. Last but not least, apply mindful listening (Chapter 4) when it is the other party's turn to speak.

HONORING YOUR BOUNDARIES

Frequently, anger tells us when our boundaries have been violated.[7]

Here is a time when I felt that my boundaries were violated and the conversation that transpired between Ally and me:

> Me: Ally, I feel a little upset that you left your cup and plate out, even though I reminded you to put them away. Will you put them away please?
>
> Ally: Okay, Mom. (She pats her little forehead lightly to show she heard me and wants to remember and puts her cup and plate away.)

---

7   Rutledge, "Got Boundaries?"

In this example, I showed respect to my emotional boundary and communicated with my daughter respectfully. The undesirable behavior was replaced with a desirable behavior without much hassle. Yes, you may create boundaries even with trivial things as such, when that thing triggers negative emotions in you.

Here is how you can determine and respect your own emotional boundaries:

- **Self-expression:** Am I seen and heard? Are we using adequate eye contact? Are we taking turns to exchange viewpoints?

- **Stability/security:** Do I feel safe emotionally and physically? Do I have an appropriate personal space?

- **Contribution and connection to self and others:** Am I contributing and connecting with the person in front of me? Are we able to agree to disagree? Am I listening to him/her attentively?

THREE QUESTIONS FOR STAYING ROOTED

Heraclitus said, "Change is the only constant in life." While things around us are moving up and down, left and right, in all directions, our emotions and physiological states are changing moment by moment too. Being aware of and accepting change is the only constant in life that can help us embrace change more and see the benefits of being more mindful and staying rooted. Hence, knowing who we are and having clarity of why we do what we do become increasingly important for us. Otherwise, we may easily be swayed by the external environment and changes come and go. These three questions help you stay rooted, as you know that you are worthy, you are living in your authentic expression, and you are nurturing and caring your mind, body, and soul, and keeping them connected as one true self.

Staying Rooted and Grounded in an Ever-Changing Environment

Do I Believe I Am Worthy (of Love)?

It is an important question for me to have an honest look at myself. From there, I can then honor who I truly am and explore where I want to lead my life. I started to have a glimpse of how low my self-worth was when I attended a personal development course. I got to discover my blind spot (*I do not deserve love*). When I was a teenager, I felt like I was either anxious or easily agitated, which I could not explain. I would choose to hang out with friends, stay back in the school to practice Chinese modern dance, etc. I did not pay attention to my siblings, and I was upset whenever my mother spoke to me. She would either ask me to do housework or attend to my siblings. I only discovered why I behaved this way in my late thirties and connected to a self-limiting belief that *I do not deserve love*. As soon as I realized this, I invited my parents and engaged them in a very vulnerable conversation over dinner. I told my parents that I was sorry, and I finally realized how much they loved me in the past. It was just my own interpretation of their love because I had a self-limiting belief that *I do not deserve love* since my teenage years. I am the eldest child among five children my parents have. Most of the attention goes to my younger siblings. When we were younger, I had to help out with taking care of my siblings, even though my own needs had not been met. Hence, subconsciously, I interpreted, *I do not deserve love*. With this self-limiting belief in my mind, it created two versions of me.

One version was *I do not deserve love, and please do not pretend that you love me. It is all lies!* This worked against my ability to believe I am loved or receive love from people around me.

The second version was *I want to be loved; I will be a good girl to have you see me, hear me, and give me love. I will be a good girl; I will do well in school; I will do well at work; please love me.*

To be able to declare, *Yes, I am worthy (of love)!* requires you to fully accept who you are and who you are not. To do so, you may be curious about yourself and personal growth. You may attempt to stop your emotional pain and decide to courageously choose to heal your inner wounds (Chapter 2). At the same time, if you have collected your personalities in the album (Chapter 3), do identify which personalities are consistently bringing emotional pain to you, and decide what you would like to do about them.

Am I Living My Truth?

What is living my truth? Having recovered my "true self" through practicing Conscious Parenting and meditation, and healing my wounded inner child, I feel "real" through my body, as I become more sensitive in paying attention to my body sensations and the flow of inner energy. I experience and believe in contentment and genuine connection. I value freedom of creative expression supported by conscious choice. I stop beating myself up when I do not achieve enough according to someone else's standards, I also become more compassionate toward myself when I observe my critical, judgmental, and overly confirming voices. I embrace my imperfection while seeing it as a beauty for me to enjoy myself more. For instance, at times, my false self may criticize how slow I am in making decisions while this may go against the pace of modern society; however, I see the beauty in allowing myself to sit with the options when I do not have clarity in deciding the best option. While allowing time and space for my inner wisdom to lead, I get to see how some of these options may be interconnected, and new options may pop up. This new discovery amazes me and gives me an extra boost of confidence to take action. This aligns with what we discussed in Chapter 2 on feeling real in true self or inner child, "the ultimately alive, energetic, receptive, creative, and fulfilled" part of our psyche. I have grown and gained so much from Conscious Parenting, I want to bring this possibility to you, who may be self-parenting or parenting others, and for you to consider this process for yourself, so that you can free your inner child and enjoy your children and build a more intimate relationship with yourself.

If I am not living my truth, I would look at what resources are available for me to do so. Look into your social networks, how you earn and spend money, how you spend your time, the opportunities you have, etc.

Family is a support system for success and a safe haven for failure, just like the sun, water, and soil a plant needs to grow. Along my journey to become a family life educator and parenting coach, my husband and my daughter are always there for me when I need to prepare for my workshops and need them to be my "pretend audience." My dad and mom are always there to ask if I need any financial support. My siblings are my sounding board when I have new ideas and provide me feedback on my talks and sharings. My in-laws are always there at least once a year to have meals together. My partners or colleagues who are aware of my social mission are there to hold me accountable for my growth and actualize my mission. While recognizing my resources, I am also feeling grateful to have such a support system to keep me going. Do you have a family support system that holds you accountable for living your truth?

Do I Take Care of My Mind, Body, and Soul?

To keep me going and to energize me each and every day, my daily practice always starts with a meditation or a thought-provoking talk from a podcast or YouTube video. Recently, I have picked up some spiritual practices that help me to be more connected to my soul purpose and get me rooted. From there, I can be more present to bring my true self to life, and to live from my connected heart, body, and soul. If you find that your mind is speaking louder and louder, that may get you stuck; please take time to bring awareness to your body and the inner energy, and feel aliveness within you. When you sense that you are not paying attention to your body sensations as often as you would like, please take time to sit with yourself and connect with your body. Consider tapping into dance or movement for mind–body connection, because how we feel in our brain affects how our body feels. Additionally, through daily meditation practice, we also practice self-acceptance or letting go of "self." When we use our breath to harness the power of patience, we reach the state of not-self; we get to connect with our higher self or soul (Chapter 2).

When you reflect on the above three areas, you are looking at yourself inside the mirror with the feeling of familiarity and congruence. At the same time, you feel supported even though you may discover your sadness, fear, frustration, stuckness, and more every now and then. However, you will not feel defeated or helpless and you can still look into the mirror and tell yourself this:

> I accept that I am stuck right now; I can feel my fear. I can invite these emotions to sit with me. I will stay rooted and listen to my heart and body before I make any decisions. One thing I am very sure of is that I will make responsible choices moving forward. Whatever mistakes I make are just my learning opportunities, and at the end of the day, I know everything is going to be okay.

six

STAYING GROUNDED
AND CENTERED

———

Because of the love I have received unconditionally from my little girl, Ally, and the work I do to become a conscious parent—heal my wounds, become a conscious observer, which allows me to choose my action from the place of love, and to honor my being over my doing—I finally get connected with my true self. My true self, who did not give up, can come out from deep inside me, and be heard and seen by me, even after my ego or false self was so strong and loud. This ability to distinguish the voices either from the true or false self, authentic self, or egoic self, has enabled me to make good choices when I was lost at times.

NOT EASILY SWAYED WHEN DIFFERENT VOICES ARE COMING AT YOU

The same ability has helped me to be present with my clients and parents I was coaching, and catch myself when I was in my ego's judgmental voices. Here are the examples of the voices from my false or ego self, usually from the place of fear, that tend to be judgmental or get to be right, and my true or authentic self, usually from the place of love, that tend to embrace the as-is or expansive:

False self's judgmental voice: I see what happened now. I want to bring (my client) to this place, and she would be able to set herself free from this entanglement if she just follows where I guide her. (From the place of fear that I may not create much value for my client, hence, there is too much focus to bring her to where I think she will benefit from this session.)

True self's embracing voice: I see where (my client) is coming from. She is so courageous to get to where she is right now; I trust that she is going to get to where she wants to be. Let us find out together if she is ready to move forward, or if she needs more support to be where she is now. (From the place of love to empower my client, so that she has the space to pace herself as she needs, and to trust her inner wisdom will bring her to where she needs to be right now.)

I am honored to have opportunities to work with some courageous souls, parents who are willing to be curiously exploring their inner world and thinking, *Maybe I am the one who needs to "grow" from here...* During the coaching sessions, I am their mirror, and they are mine. As presently as I can, I am a good observer and listen to myself while holding space for my clients. Here are some collective pains and strengths of our growing journey together.

SARAH'S STORY: I WANT MY CHILD TO HAVE A BETTER CHILDHOOD THAN MINE!

Sarah separated from her husband and wanted to build a closer relationship with her son. During the coaching sessions, she got that her ego and guilt were standing between her and her son and distancing their relationship. Sarah wanted to make up with her son so badly, hoping to give him the best of everything. At the same time, she faced the guilt of not being able to provide for him a two-parent family.

At a deeper level, because she did not have attentive parents during her childhood, and her dearest brother passed away when she was nine years old, no one was available for her to help her grieve. She was longing for a reliable man who adored her just like her brother to reappear in her life. Whenever she felt helpless and alone, it reminded her of the loneliness she experienced after her brother left her. The more she wanted to provide for her son, the more she felt guilty. She could not focus

198   PARENTING UNCHAINED

on the child in front of her or honor the strengths in her child. She clung to her pain and felt stuck. She told me at the end of the session that she could not control her emotions in front of her son, as deep inside, she always felt that some part of her was missing and she would not be a good enough mother.

Early in the coaching journey, at some sessions, Sarah was able to align with her inner strength and hold the power to connect with her child and attune to his needs. She could detach from her emotional baggage and observe her thoughts. At other sessions, she would join the coaching sessions in "I am the victim" mode, believing that there was nothing she could do that would improve her relationship with her son. Along this healing journey, she practiced Wu Tao Dance Therapy, listened to the teachings and did home assignments during workshops, participated in group discussions, scheduled one-on-one coaching as and when required, and practiced Conscious Parenting skills during her daily interaction with her son. Beside the mentioned structure that we set up, she would also be prompted to check in with herself and look for cues that indicated her resistance to change or detect her old patterns that were trying to keep her within her comfort zone.

Face Avoidance

Through the coaching sessions, we started reading into her habits and areas of avoidance that did not serve her. We paid extra attention to things that she was aware of where she needed to take action, but she was not moving a tiny step forward and kept coming back to dwelling on herself. That was where we discovered that she was unconsciously avoiding being left alone again. This was also affecting her relationship with her son as she wanted to be by her son's side and did her best to give him a loving environment growing up, but many times, this "loving" environment suffocated her son.

Here are some examples of behaviors for you to identify to check if you are gravitating toward avoidance:

- You do not have the *drive* to get up in the morning. You are probably still keeping your routine; however, the spark and excitement are fading.

- You lose your *spark* and *momentum* in completing your daily work, and you are postponing or rescheduling your tasks and meetings for the day and telling yourself that you will get to them later.

- You would rather spend time with yourself doing nothing, or you desperately look for external distractions to avoid dealing with, or covering up, what is happening inside you. You do this by watching TV, browsing your social media posts or YouTube videos, playing video games, eating unconsciously to fill up your emotional emptiness, asking different people out for a chat or a drink, etc. All these behaviors "support" you to escape from your unease or emptiness within. If you go inward, you may also notice that this unease and emptiness drains your energy and exhausts you, even if you choose to do nothing.

Be aware when you are in the mode of avoidance. Remind yourself that you may escape from inner unease or emptiness for the time being, but what you are avoiding may not go away until you are attending to or taking care of the pain. Some may even say to you, "Time can heal." However, I hope you have already noticed time cannot heal everything. Incidents, things, people, and/or relationships you need to learn and grow up from will keep showing up until you have truly learned from them.

In addition, you may find you are resisting healthy and supportive relationships. Are your relationships with your loved ones out of alignment with your inner truth?

- Outside of you, you might feel you cannot maintain any good relationships around you, from children, spouses, and coworkers to your business partners, extended family, and friends.

- If you were to look deeper inside with honesty, you could gather that you might be more self-centered and could not and would not be willing to pay attention to the needs of your children, spouse, family members, or anyone else during this down time.

- You know you should not behave a certain way, but you just cannot control your emotional reactions.

- In your relationship with yourself, you might feel suffocated or trapped internally and be judgmental toward yourself and others.

Instead of having your fingers pointed outward to others, giving your power to others to control your experiences with these relationships, please be reminded that you play a part in building and maintaining these relationships. As long as you have built a solid relationship with yourself, naturally and unavoidably, you are bringing that love and kindness you have given to yourself to others too. I would like to share a quote from Dr. Shefali Tsabary. I relate to it and have shared it countless times during my parenting talks and workshops. "Every interaction with our children is a direct reflection of our own relationship with ourselves."

If you have found yourself heading toward these pitfalls, what can you do when you have found yourself getting into the spiraling cycle of avoidance?

- Be aware of when you are in the mode of avoidance. Your sympathetic nervous system within the autonomic nervous system is keeping you safe from exposure to new "risks" or "changes," or interpreting them as "danger."[1]

---

1 Porges, "Polyvagal Theory"; Cleveland Clinic, "Autonomic Nervous System."

Hence, it is holding you back, and sending you back to your comfort zone.

- Have self-compassion and acknowledge that you cannot always regulate yourself well and adjust to the new normal quickly, but you can tell yourself, "It is my life! I can bring back the power to choose how I live my life."

- Check in with yourself. Most likely your relationship with yourself is out of inner alignment. Go to the section "Unchaining Your Old Patterns by Practicing SPHERIC" and apply the "Bring Me Home" tool later in this chapter to bring yourself back to your home, your core.

- Appreciate the fact that you can live in the present moment, and ask what you can do now that can contribute to the person or situation in front of your eyes.

- A new normal requires you to establish new routines or new habits. Take small steps to restart. Stick to your new intention to want to change your old ways of living and being, include meditation practice in your daily routine, and realign yourself with your life goals.

Conscious Self-Parenting and Reflection

Have you done a SMART goal-setting exercise before? Take the following life goal setting exercise as an example, and create one for yourself. Why is it important to create life goals? It gives you a sense of direction of the kind of

life you are moving toward, day in and day out. It gives you motivation and reasons to wake up in the morning, progresses throughout the day, puts a sense of meaning within you before you go to sleep, and faces avoidance when it hits you. It helps you pull people, ideas, perspectives, resources, and strengths together to get you going day after day.

- Create or revise your life goals, and we will integrate with the upcoming section "Establishing Your Daily Reflection System" and support you to actualize and realign yourself with your life goals regularly. Suggested areas of life goals to think about are:
  - Self-Development and Self-Care
  - Parent–Child Relationship
  - Career/Expanding Social Networks
  - Spouse/Parents Relationship

- You are also welcome to create a vision board and write a short summary of different areas of your life goals, just to spark an idea for the start (e.g., self-development and self-care). On your vision board, you may include images such as your favorite exercises, healthier choices of food, your hobbies, your spiritual wellness preferences, etc.

Here is a sample of the short summary, "To cultivate my holistic well-being, from physical, intellectual, emotional, and social to spiritual wellness. For physical, I am going to schedule a five-minute dance with my favorite music, or at times, invite Ally to dance with me with her favorite music for bonding too." As you are breaking the goals down, you can set specific actions or activities or tasks to help you to get there. From specific items, you can organize them into a daily checklist for you to take action.

PERSONAL LiFE GOALS
DAILY CHECKLIST

(1) SELF-DEVELOPMENT & SELF-CARE
- [ ] STAY CALM THROUGH TAKING THREE DEEP BREATHS
- [ ] SLEEP BY 10PM, SLEEP FOR 7–8HRS
- [ ] LISTEN TO ONE AUDIO BOOK A MONTH
- [ ] CONSUME LESS SUGAR
- [ ] EAT RAINBOW-COLORED FOOD
- [ ] KEEP A DEVICE-FREE BEDROOM
- [ ] PRIORITISE, END PROCRASTINATION DO FUN STUFF
- [ ] RESTORE ENERGY AND PRACTICE SELF-LOVE

(2) PARENT-CHILD RELATIONSHIP
- [ ] EXPECT LESS, LOVE MORE
- [ ] PRACTICE EMOTIONAL REGULATIONS
- [ ] SPEAK FROM HEART, NOT FROM HEAD
- [ ] HAVE FUN WHILE SPENDING QUALITY TIME WITH KID

(3) SPOUSE/ PARENTS RELATIONSHIP
- [ ] HEAL TOGETHER FROM CHALLENGING TIME
- [ ] CHOOSE LOVE

(4) CAREER / EXPANDING SOCIAL NETWORKS
- [ ] FOLLOW WISDOM TEACHERS
- [ ] WORK WITH PARTNERS WHO HOLD SIMILAR MISSION
- [ ] ATTEND SOMATIC EXPERIENCING PROFESSIONAL TRAINING

I noticed a similar mode of avoidance was flowing through me when I was building my parenting coaching business and when I was writing my book. I had set a goal for my coaching business and had a plan to connect with three of my friends or my friends' friends who are mothers daily for a month. My intention was to find out how they were coping with their parent–child relationship, to share with them what Conscious Parenting means, and to ask if they saw how this might be helpful for them at the moment. I had laid the tasks out in my online calendar; however, I saw myself falling into the similar pattern of postponing the calls, gave myself excuses for not making those calls, and went into my comfort zone again. It was to keep myself "safe" in a familiar environment and continue to stand still at the same old place. I could see my fear of stepping out of my comfort zone. Nonetheless, I had to transit through and move my new pursuit and intention into the new normal. I started taking baby steps:

- I told myself that it was going to be alright, it was a tiny step, it was nothing too daunting, and I just started with connecting with one parent at a time.

- I could see the more I was avoiding, the more I clung onto the thought of me resisting my avoidance and self-doubt (e.g., "Why can I not honor my word?").

- I told myself that there would be no tomorrow, as I would not know what would happen tomorrow, I might not be around, I might have other things to attend to, my day might have some "surprises" or last-minute things to attend to, etc. At the very least, I still had today.

- I needed to strike the balance of pushing myself out of my comfort zone. At the same time, I would not scare myself away from confronting this fear. When I got stuck, to do the balancing act, I would first try to push myself a little to get out of my comfort zone. However, at times, I would be running out of energy. I would then accept, right there, that I would prefer to stay within my comfort zone. I would try again after some rest and or recharging.

If my mode of avoidance persists on other occasions, I check in with myself and see if I am out of my inner alignment. I may apply "Bring Me Home" in this chapter and explore the source of avoidance, which I may revisit in Chapter 2 or Chapter 3.

ESTABLISHING YOUR DAILY REFLECTION SYSTEM

Furthermore, I have also set up a system to help support and live the life we want, and to hold ourselves accountable for daily progress, while at the same time, to celebrate what I have done well or to be grateful about the learning opportunities presented, even though they may be challenging or difficult at the beginning. Here are some details of the daily reflection system.

Regular Reflection and Gratitude Journal

- Reflect on what you are grateful for the day, and what you want to take different action(s) on from today forward.

- Be nonjudgmental about your thoughts. If it is too hard, just notice you are judging your thoughts (e.g., good or bad). You can choose to amplify the good ones or dim the bad ones, or choose not to do anything about them. Yes, choose not to do anything about them. It is not about letting the bad ones erode you; you are just accepting the bad ones. When you are ready, you may reframe and transform the bad ones into the good and be guided by your inner wisdom. How would you know whether these good ones come from wisdom? When they are not from the place of fear, you know you are not trying to control the others or the outcomes; you are honoring these good decisions and feeling grateful about the outcomes.

- Most importantly, because of your good thoughts, you have the power to transform the bad ones. Using a moon eclipse as the metaphor, as the shadows blacken the moon, you are able to focus on the bright side of the moon, which are good thoughts. You can hold the space for the shadows and embrace the darkness as you see the beauty and warmth of the bright eclipse. You are going to recognize the beauty in these shadows, because without them, the eclipse light is not going to be seen as bright as it should be. By practicing gratitude, we are likely to be able to transform an obstacle into an opportunity.

There is a fine line though. You need to be mindful about not using gratitude to numb yourself and talk yourself into saying, "Anyway, life has given me so much, I cannot complain more, but to give in to what has happened to me." Coupling mindfulness meditation with gratitude as a regular practice may help keep your perspective balanced, such as asking yourself the following questions used from *three questions of Naikan* therapy:

- What have I received from __ (e.g., this person or event)?
- What have I given to __ (e.g., this person or event)?
- What troubles and difficulties have I caused __ (e.g., this person or event)?

There are many more ways to strengthen your gratitude muscle. You may refer to Dr. Robert Emmons's everyday tips for living a life of gratitude (see the "Tools & Resources" section).

Since my daughter, Ally, was seven, I have created this ritual within my family every Saturday night. We talk about what we are grateful for about one another for the week. Usually we will start from the youngest to the oldest, from Ally to my husband, Ivan. One of these gratitude nights, Ally thanked me for preparing her favorite food while I thanked her for taking in that particular week like it was a perfect week for her, and appreciating the dinners, even with the less-than-perfect over-cooked fish. Ally thanked her father for chauffeuring her from school to her dance lessons despite his busy work schedule. Other examples of the gratitudes she gave her father were buying her durians and they were so yummy, and speaking to her teacher about things she forgot to do, etc.[2] He thanked Ally for making him some tasty chocolate chip cookies, etc. I thanked my husband for giving me space to do things I was passionate about, mainly parenting coaching, the Nannies on Wheels social enterprise project, and teaching part-time without rushing me to get back to my full-time job, which is not a social norm here in Singapore, as the majority of married couples are dual-career couples.[3] Other times I was grateful that he drove us from Singapore to Malaysia and bought my parents dinner so that we could spend quality time with them. He thanked me for taking care of and cooking for Ally that week when he was having some important meetings. More than frequently, the adults (my husband and I) would add "but," like how we process our thoughts automatically on things we could have done better. We did set a rule for not adding "but," as it would complicate our feelings of gratitude toward one another, such as the person who is receiving gratitude would be confused whether we are grateful or not.

---

2   The "king of fruits," the durian is distinctive for its large size, strong odor, and thorn-covered rind.

3   Ho, "More Dual-Income Couples in S'pore."

Morning Meditation and Reset

This has been a daily practice of mine. I usually wake up at six in the morning; I do some movements first and then proceed with a forty-five-minute silent meditation. With this routine, I am able to keep a calm and clear mind for the entire day.

Here is how you approach it:

- Sit with yourself and connect from within.
- Take three deep breaths.
- Tell yourself, "I am starting a brand-new day!"
- Mentally scan your body and notice if there is any tension.
- You can choose to release the tension by taking a deep breath in, releasing tension as you breathe out. Repeat a few times or just be aware of it.
- Start from your head, then move your focus to your face, your shoulders, your hands, your fingers, your chest, your stomach, your hips, your lap, your knees, your shins, and your feet.
- Focus on your breathing.
- When you realize you are aware that your focal point is away from your breaths, bring yourself back through breathing, and be aware you are right here and now. Or you may also follow the steps of the breathing technique provided in Chapter 2.

As you are on the go during the day, and you find yourself getting distracted easily, you are welcome to focus on your mindful breathing. Bring yourself back to your breaths; notice your in-and-out breaths, even with your eyes open, when you are in the midst of your conversations, driving, walking, doing housework, etc.

Daily Intention Setting

Create an intention on an overarching attitude you want to lead your life for the day using representational systems or sensory systems such as listening. While we are setting high-level life goals, we are setting specific objectives that help us move toward our life goals day by day, putting the plan into action, listening attentively to our internal voices or self-talks, while filtering external voices or noises. For instance, I have been setting daily intentions since 2014 with a group of my leadership accountability buddies. One of the examples of my daily intention setting is "I create aliveness. Listening from self-compassion." This intention has set the "tone" or quality of the day that I wish to achieve. As I am on the go throughout the day, I may check in and realign with myself by listening to my inner voices or filtering voices that do not serve me. In other words, whether or not the first intention of the day can last for the whole day, it gets us thinking about how we want to live our life for that day and reminds us to be the leader of our life.

Goals Setting: Two Yeses and One No

Earlier in this chapter, we have a reflection and self-parenting practice to create or revise our life goals, which set up a direction for us to achieve things that are important to us in this lifetime. Those are your long-term goals; you may chunk them down into short-term goals or smaller tasks for you to work toward your long-term goals year after year, month after month, or even day after day. When I am bringing the smaller tasks into my Daily Intention Setting, I will observe what is working and what is not working. While saying yes to proceed and execute them daily, I will also remove or modify what is not working for me.

For instance, I wish to introduce families with different perspectives and options for raising their children; this is my long-term goal. To do so, I will create different parenting programs that speak to parents. Setting this goal with SMART criteria, this is how it is going to look when the action is *I will make a complimentary call appointment with a friend daily to share about self-parenting (nonparent) or Conscious Parenting (parent):*[4]

- Short-term goals
  - Yes, to accept a complimentary call appointment with a friend daily

---

4   CFI Team, "SMART Goals."

- Yes, to create a post to four key social media circles (e.g., one post every three days on Facebook, Instagram, LinkedIn, and WeChat)
- No, to accept more than two complimentary call appointments per day

- Long-term goals
  - To build solid, trustworthy, and authentic coach–client relationships as a self-parenting/parenting coach and family life educator that empowers parents
  - To be a courageous and committed conscious mother who parents herself first before parenting her child

Regularly, to keep the life goals alive, a regular stocktaking will help. For instance, to schedule and revisit all short-term goals every three months, I will honestly look at what works and what does not work in order to achieve my long-term goals. Then, I will create new and/or modify short-term goals, after realigning them with long-term goals.

Take Action

Record your action items on the calendar and take action. I have all my action items reserved in my electronic calendar. Before I got myself unchained from old patterns and habits through parenting, I used to feel pressured for not attending to my action items according to plan. I would put myself down for procrastination. Now that I have unchained my childhood wounds and parented myself into self-growth and personal development, I make plans more realistically. It takes much commitment and honesty to tell myself I am not here to please others, and most importantly, not to please or lie to myself, but something I can and will attend to are these tasks on my calendar. One would not be able to shift or remove his or her old patterns and habits overnight. I approach my day by doing two to three things that help me head toward my long-term goal and removing one thing from my list at the end of every week that does not serve me anymore.

Awakening your aliveness does not only remind you to live the life you want to have; it also reminds you that you can become more aware of giving space and learning opportunities for your child(ren) to keep their aliveness and truth as much as they can.

Once upon a time, I was a timid growing child and reserved young adult who yearned for my parents' approval. I was not awakened until I became a mother, after interpreting and receiving my daughter's unconditional love toward me. Since then, I have shed my protective layer/armor to "fight against" intrusion from others, keep my avoidance alongside with me, and stop running away from facing my fear and uncovering my veil of not-good-enoughness. When I do not have an answer within me, or when I am unsure of what to do next, I will pause and stay with the uneasy feelings, and I am ready to take a step further. Life becomes simpler and more straightforward as long as I focus on the present moment and feel my aliveness.

Conscious Self-Parenting and Reflection

- Describe a time you truly felt grateful to be alive by simply enjoying the simplest thing in life.
- What do you do to remind yourself of your pure aliveness? Some examples are:
  - Hug a tree: put your ear closer to the tree trunk and listen to nature.
  - Dance along with your favorite music.
  - I learned this from Ally when she was a toddler. She was fascinated by ants. As I followed her line of sight, she was watching ants' ongoing searching for or carrying food. I remembered once she was crying at the park because she was not ready to go home for dinner. I saw a colony of ants and distracted her from crying, and told her they were going home, and so must we. ☺ Please be encouraged to learn from your young children how they simply enjoy life in the present moment.

UNCHAINING YOUR OLD PATTERNS BY PRACTICING SPHERIC

The "breaking SPHERIC chain" tool starts you with key questions to carry on your inner dialogue further; you can practice it as daily reflection. This tool has helped me in connecting with myself, and brought me back to my inner alignment. At a psychological level, we generally run our life in two modes: (1) I am the author of my life, and I run my life; (2) I am the victim of life, and I am run by life. What do your inner monologues sound like from moment to moment each day?

Practicing SPHERIC

SPHERIC	Description
Spicing	Spicing up life through what we do
Performing	Performing tasks to achieve short- or long-term goal(s)
Honoring	Honoring my own uniqueness and strengths, and actualizing life goals
Embracing	Embracing change, mistakes, etc., and continuing to grow and learn
Recharging	Restoring energy and moving forward
Intention setting	Setting intention for the day, realigning what you do with your intention at the end of the day, living life the way you want it to be
Clearing	Clearing and emptying a mind full of stress, negativity, and judgment

I have included what my own practice of SPHERIC would look like on the following page. You are welcome to give it a try and mix and match SPHERIC according to your own needs because this is a very personalized process. You will have your own "secret ingredients/processes" that work for you and only you.

As you become more familiar with SPHERIC, you can break them up into pieces, mix and match the seven pieces, and apply one or more, moment by moment as you need. Your mixed-and-matched pieces and personalized SPHERIC tool may look like this. You are free to customize your processes and invent your own memorable mnemonics.

YOUR OWN SPHERIC
DAILY ROUTINE

MORNING

Doing meditation
Clearing and emptying my mind, getting closer with my inner truth through connecting with my body. Receiving information via body sensation and mind interpretation.

Dancing Wu Tao (Dance Therapy)
Mind and body wellness, with the dance movement and music, Wu Tao dance stimulates energy flow through my corresponding organs and meridian system.

During mid-day, Wu Tao dance helps me replenish and recharge my energy and relax my mind, body, and soul.

(You may also replace other self-care or calming exercises or activities.)

Journaling
Journaling helps me to get clear with my thoughts, detach my emotions, and get clarity where I truly want to lead my life.

Additionally, I can also do **intention setting** for the day: who I want to be, what I need to do, and what I need to say so that I can live the way I wish life to be.

WORKING HOURS

Working
Performing and achieving goals, and being an observer of myself and my own responses toward events, places, things, people, etc.

Honoring my uniqueness and my strengths.

Embracing changes and mistakes.

Spicing up work, and using a sense of humor to resolve conflicts.

EVENING

Connecting with family & friends
Clearing what happened at work, Honoring my family members, friends, colleagues for their time and contributions to the meet-up.

Spicing up my moments spending time with my family and friends.

Resting and being grateful
Embracing everything happened for the day.

Clearing a head full of matters from the day and work.

"Pluck and Play" SPHERIC in Your Daily Routine

ICE

(Intention Setting. Clearing. Embracing.)—Morning Starter

You can ICE your morning by starting with intention setting, clearing, and emptying your judgment and unhealthy thoughts. Keep your cool and start a fresh day! Remind yourself that you can embrace changes and mistakes coming at you during the day or embrace yourself should you make mistakes or not meet your expectation at your first attempt in things you do.

PHI-RES

(Performing. Honoring. Intention Setting.
Recharging. Embracing. Spicing—
Sounds like "Fires.")—Fire Up during the Day

During the day, you perform your tasks, honor your strengths, and align with your intention set for the day. Recharge yourself with breathing or grounding exercises, embrace things that may or may not turn out the way you want them to be. Spice your activities and actions a little, and make them enjoyable and fun for you and people involved.

CHERISH

(Clearing. Honoring. Recharging. Intention Setting.
Spicing.)—Cherish What You Have Gotten

To wrap up for the day in the evening, and spend time with yourself or family, you can *clear* and empty any negativity that may still remain in your thoughts. *Honor* what you have accomplished for the day, *embrace* all your emotions. *Recharge* yourself with a healthy meal or a relaxed shower, etc. Revisit your *intention set* and show up in front of your loved ones. *Spice up* your evening with a few favorite activities such as family games, reading, etc. and ease yourself and loved ones before going to bed. Wrap up your day by *honoring* your effort and penning your gratitude in a journal.

CHLOE'S STORY: I AM BRINGING UP MY TWINS ALONE

Chloe was a mother to her four-year-old twin daughters. She felt lonely raising her daughters, even though her husband was by their sides. She could not feel the support and warmth from her spouse. She felt her in-laws were against her, nearly causing her to lose her job. She believed that she was raising her twins alone and kept a distance from her family. Should she take the courage to clarify with her in-laws, speak her truth, be authentic and vulnerable to first seek to understand then be understood, she might have a different family dynamic. She might have a team to raise her twins together.

What would it take for her to build up that courage? She could start from the place of loving herself:

1. She could honestly express her vulnerability, "I do not know where to start; however, my intention comes from a place of love."

2. She could describe what happened and how it made her feel, and share her own observation about the other party without judging or drawing a conclusion about her spouse and in-laws. She could give them space to share their piece from their perspectives. When both parties were being heard, that was where the communication started. If she found it difficult for her to sit calmly and hold this communication, she could also consider

looping in a third neutral party who would be a trusted figure by both sides.

3. When it was their turn to speak, she could provide deep listening and compassion. She could hold the space for other parties while they were expressing how they felt, as well as for herself, and not forget to keep breathing.

4. She could negotiate a win–win for both parties. Keeping in mind that the common goal would be for the best interest of the children, both parties could find common ground and build consensus.

The above would be a way to get oneself heard, and show up for oneself, and stand from the truth. Chloe could "pluck and play" SPHERIC as such to assist and bring her back to her core and intention to hold this family conversation. She would apply it as such:

- **H**—Honor the other parties who are willing to take time to take part in the family meeting or conversation.
- **E**—Embrace all emotions that surfaced, and consciously choose not to react, but to be her own observer.
- **I**—Align with her intention set for the meeting or conversation.
- **R**—Recharge herself before the meeting, so that she would be less affected by any mental or physical exhaustion.

Conscious Self-Parenting and Reflection

Integrate SPHERIC into your daily life, align and realign your intention during the day, honor your strengths to perform well in your tasks to achieve your goals, clear unwanted noises and energy that create barriers, embrace mistakes or imperfections, spice up and enjoy the working process and human-to-human interaction during your day.

Time	Activity	Practice SPHERIC
Morning	e.g., doing meditation	
	e.g., calming activities or exercises	
	e.g., journaling	
Working hours	e.g., working	
Evening	e.g., connecting with family and friends	
	e.g., resting and being grateful	

SPHERIC supports you to flow through your everyday life. The following tool, "Bring Me Home," provides you another angle, or entry points, to get to know you and connect with yourself. There may be times that you find intention setting not aligned with your action, or for those who are more sensitive to your body sensations, you might find your mind and body sending conflicting messages (e.g., you might be very committed to working toward your goal and action plan; however, you are not putting your plan into action). Your mind is telling you one thing, and your body is doing another. Hence, you will apply the "Bring Me Home" self-check-in to find gaps in your inner alignment, tweak your intention setting, perform different tasks, honor what you have done well, and/or embrace areas you need to improve in SPHERIC.

1. **Who am I?**
   - **I think I am...**
     Example: I'm a curious human being.
   - **How I behave shows what I think...**
     I have been curiously exploring my possibilities by attending different experiential workshops, and learning something new about myself.
     Example: Yesterday, I was presented with an opportunity by a stranger. I did not reject it right away, I observed we have different energy levels, I thought she could help push me moving forward.
   - **As I check in with my body, I feel both what I think and how I behave are aligned, or not...**

While I wish I could have the power of execution, having sat with myself and checked in with my body, I decided to stay with my core strengths, and let things unfold one step at a time, along with my readiness in moving along. In short, through curiosity I attended new workshops, obtained new knowledge, and met new people. I felt inner alignment continue to guide me to take new value-based action.

2. **What do I stand for?**
   - **I think I stand for…**
     Example: I stand for love and compassion.
   - **How I behave shows what I think…**
     Ever since I have tasted the power of authenticity, and to be true to myself, I have shared and emphasized the same—It is important to be honest and true to ourselves, also as a role model for my daughter.

     Example: Yesterday, I found out the iPad was placed in between the calendar stands on her study table. I told her straight that I need to move the iPad to the living room, so that we could cut down on distractions. She whispered into my ear and said, "Mommy, I have been honest to myself. I did not touch my iPad all this while."

     As a conscious parent, I have always put love and compassion as the primary ingredients in building

"BRING ME HOME"
CONNECT WITH YOURSELF FROM WITHIN

I think I am...

① Who am I?

How I behave shows what I think...

As I check in with my body, I feel both what I think and how I behave are aligned, or not...

I think I stand for...

How I behave shows what I think...

② What do I stand for?

As I check in with my body, I feel both what I think and how I behave are aligned, or not...

(continued on next page)

"BRING ME HOME"
CONNECT WITH YOURSELF FROM WITHIN

I think my attitude is...

How I behave shows what I think...

③ What is my attitude toward life at the present moment?

My attitude in life = What I think + What I do + How I feel

As I check in with my body, I feel both what I think and how I behave are aligned, or not...

I think my attitude toward my children is...

④ What is my attitude toward my children?

My attitude in life = How I feel + What I do + What my belief is

How I behave shows what I think...

As I check in with my body, I feel both what I think and how I behave are aligned, or not...

my relationship with my daughter. I can see how it
pays off over time.

- **As I check in with my body, I feel both what I think
  and how I behave are aligned, or not...**
  I stand for love and compassion. I do as I say by
  showing love and passion to people around me.

  I sensed inner alignment from this incident. I felt
  grateful to hear that she was honest with herself.

  I believe she can trust herself more, just like I
  have experienced the same within me, over time.

3. **What is my attitude toward life at the present moment?**
   - **My attitude in life = What I think + What I do +
     How I feel**
   - **I think my attitude is...**
     Example: I am excited about life, as I think/believe
     it is full of opportunities, I keep trying to live a
     successful life.

     Today, I think the term "successful life" to me is
     to be able to stay in the present moment, which has
     no right/wrong, no good/bad, no judgment. This
     opens up wider possibilities in life.
   - **How I behave shows what I think...**
     I have observed that I can bring myself back to the
     center and be in the present moment daily. At times,
     I face distractions and drift away. I can choose to not
     make myself wrong, just bring myself back to "home"

(center and in the present moment), and then move on to working toward my goals one step at a time.

- **As I check in with my body, I feel both what I think and how I behave are aligned, or not...**
  When I am distracted, I tend to waste much energy in judging myself for not being able to honor my word. As I bring myself back to the present moment, I get to check in with myself, and quiet down my judging and distracted mind. As I reset, and realign with my life goals, I feel calm, and my body becomes more relaxed, and I can be productive again.

  In short, my attitude about "successful life" is to stay open to possibilities moment-by-moment. Living this attitude helps me stay open-minded in every area of my life, including parenting.

4. **What is my attitude toward my children?**
   - **My attitude in life = How I feel + What I do + What my belief is**
   - **I think my attitude toward my children is...**
     Example 1: I love my son very much. I feel angry whenever he disobeys me. I think he is a difficult child.

     "I think my son is a difficult child, hence, he makes me a difficult parent."

     Allow external factors to affect what you think, or put oneself as the victim, and give up on taking control back or taking ownership for what happened.

Example 2: I think my daughter is a precious and spiritual gift sent to me. I believe through her, I get to learn more about myself, giving me inner strengths and a deeper connection with myself.

- **How I behave shows what I think...**
  Example 1: "I am the victim of my life" mode: When my son doesn't listen to me, I get really upset, I yell at him, and sometimes, I can't help throwing things in front of him. I don't want to hit him, hence, I have decided to throw things to help release my anger.

  Example 2: "I am the author of my life" mode: Whenever I am facing setbacks, I tap on my go-to message to remind me how grateful I am to be a mother, to love and to be loved by another human being.

- **As I check in with my body, I feel both what I think and how I behave are aligned, or not...**
  Example 1: I always regret yelling at him and throwing things in front of him. I think he is a difficult child, but I love him very much. My thinking, feeling, and actions are not aligned, and I am confused.

  To be aware of how I am not aligned with how I feel, think and behave, I can choose to let go of my anger through other means. For instance, when I feel angry, I can take three deep breaths, or touch my crystal beads, instead of throwing things. I may make mistakes and throw things again when I feel angry with my son, but I love him, and I do not want him to throw things like me when he feels angry. I do as I say. I am staying away from creating mixed messages toward my son.

I choose to feel peace, and I can think of a peaceful way to release my anger.

Example 2: I feel grateful and regard my daughter as a spiritual gift for my self-growth, and can overcome any setbacks from the place of love and abundance, which is what I stand for. I can tap on my inner resources to deal with setbacks or challenges.

From the above examples, I hope you get to see that there is no particular sequence to follow; you can reflect from different entry points (i.e., "Who am I?" "What do I stand for?" "What is my attitude toward life at the present moment?" "What is my attitude toward my children?")

Conscious Self-Parenting and Reflection

*Observing Self (Stage II)—
"Bring Me Home"—Connect
with Yourself from Within*

Get to know more about yourself through observing your inner and

outer world. At the same time, through daily structure and practice, use SPHERIC to keep your mind and body or thinking and action aligned. You can even use SPHERIC to detect when you are out of alignment with your thinking and action.

"Bring Me Home"—Connect with Yourself from Within

1 Who am I?	I think I am...	How I behave shows what I think...	As I check in with my body, I feel both what I think and how I behave are aligned, or not...

2 What do I stand for?	I think I stand for...	How I behave shows what I think...	As I check in with my body, I feel both what I think and how I behave are aligned, or not...

3	**What is my attitude toward life at the present moment?** *My attitude in life = What I think + What I do + How I feel*	I think my attitude is…	How I behave shows what I think…	As I check in with my body, I feel both what I think and how I behave are aligned, or not…

4	**What is my attitude toward my children?** *My attitude in life = What I think + What I do + How I feel*	I think my attitude toward my children is…	How I behave shows what I think…	As I check in with my body, I feel both what I think and how I behave are aligned, or not…

The "Bring Me Home" tool helps us to bring ourselves back to inner alignment. On top of that, it keeps us grounded and rooted from within. You can stay mindful and be the observer of life with the presence of heart; it gives you a sense of mind-body-soul connection.

KEEPING THE CHANGE WITHIN ME

Once you are able to keep the change, sustain at the stage pursuing your personal growth, and reach your highest self, you will never turn back. Along with my awakened journal, these were three of the hardest things to do:

1. To start from ground zero, accept my bad not-enoughness, and acknowledge that I am a whole and complete human being.

2. To embrace others' differences and be compassionate about how others are just not aware of better ways to deal with their negative feelings, emotions, stuckness, etc. Therefore, I could be looped into their emotional spirals. How do I stay grounded for myself and be compassionate enough to hold the space for others to get through their "bad inner weather"?

3. To recognize that all mistakes and negativities are learning opportunities; we encounter them for good reasons.

My self-parenting and discovery journey might not have happened if I was not curious enough about what happened inside of me when I parented my child. There were emotional pains and sufferings I kept experiencing and I could not explain the reasons for them. Back then, I was not even aware that these pains and sufferings were caused by my childhood wounds or due to my childhood needs not being met. I even thought it was my child who created these emotional pains for me. As I learned more about myself through Conscious Parenting, I got to connect my pain and suffering with my fear of my not-good-enoughness—it is how I interpreted things about myself from my childhood experiences. I only got to let go of these pains and sufferings after I embarked on my healing journey.

Our Fear of Being Rejected

There was an episode that happened between my then-eleven-year-old Ally and me. One day, during her home-based learning, I gave her a challenge for practicing self-control and managing her time spent on online games. We set a simple rule that she could play her online games for an hour as soon as she completed all her homework for the day. I was giving her space to regulate herself, so that she could improve her self-control skills. While I went into her room and brought in the robot vacuum cleaner, I saw her playing an online game. I did not say a word and continued to do my chores. I noticed she was on the game for another three times when I went into her room; I did not say a word. After some time, she came and looked for me and told me she did not think she would ever complete her homework. I could sense how frustrated she was. I was sitting beside her and giving her space to get this off her chest. I asked if she would like to listen to some options I saw that she could do moving forward.

She was open to listening. The options were: (1) we could sit down together and go through items she would be required to complete for each day; or (2) she could list them on her own, then prioritize them with me as her sounding board. She chose the latter. Having all items listed, she felt relieved. She went on and told me she could complete the remaining work for the day.

Sometime later, I asked if she completed her homework. She replied, "Almost done." Having observed another time, she was still playing online games before she completed her homework for the day, so I decided to interrupt and stop her. I was trying to hold the space and listen to her reasons for not following through the digital rule we had set. She was upset by this question and told me she needed some space. I came out from her room, sat with myself, and started reflecting on what happened. I felt I did not stand my ground firmly and did not follow through with the rule and boundary we had agreed upon on digital usage. I started hearing my inner chatter: "You were not as good as you thought you were." I had self-doubt. I caught myself projecting that to my daughter, Ally. That doubt I had for myself became the doubt I had for her. I did not trust that she could follow through on completing her homework for the day while seeing her playing games online. When she got upset and requested space, she felt my doubts toward her.

The next day, before dawn broke, I woke up naturally, and I decided to look deeper into my self-doubt. As I was going into my Inner Child Visualization meditation, I was taking a few deep breaths and connecting to my body. I did a body scan; I could feel my chest was tight. I felt heavy-hearted. As I was more present with my breaths, I started recalling the recent interaction with my daughter that triggered my big feelings. At the surface, I was anxious about "what if" my daughter could not better manage her self-control, and she would be addicted to the online game. At a deeper level, I was afraid of being rejected. I was trying out different ways to help Ally to practice self-control using digital devices and online games. And yet, at that moment, when she was getting upset and requesting, "Mommy, I need some space," I could not help but feel rejected. You may be wondering why I felt rejected when my daughter requested space from having me check on her and hold her accountable for completing her homework. There were different layers of personalities that showed up. From the outer layer, as I reflected, there was my expectation to see an immediate effect from our discussion. I was expecting Ally to honor her word and complete her homework since she said she could. I also painted a scene of her completing her homework in my head. There was a part of me that was seeking instant gratification. I could praise her for overcoming her emotional barrier. I would have a good feeling for giving her the space to regulate her own emotion and gather that both of us did well, but it did not happen right away. As I probed deeper in the inner layer, hearing "I need some space" felt like a door slammed in my face, even though I was being good and had good intention to remind her again to complete her work. I did have an intense emotion at that moment, a wound that was rediscovered through this incident.

My Wound of Being Rejected Happened during Childhood

There was a childhood incident I could vividly recall that happened when I was eight years old. I was chosen to be considered as the model student that year. The school committee gathered all representatives of model students from each class at primary two into the teachers' office. Eight students were standing in front of the teachers in the committee, they were staring at us, and one of them said, "Looking at the students, they all look like model students. Why not get them to bring in their school bags, so that we can further assess them." I joined the rest of the students, went back to my classroom and got my school bag, and returned to the teachers' room. Before I was aware of what was going on, one of the teachers in the committee took out everything in my school bag. She was flipping through my books and my belongings, and she found some of my textbooks were scribbled in. She said, "Look at what you did to your textbooks!" Before I could reply, she moved on and checked on other students. I felt unfairly and falsely accused. I muttered, "My young siblings did these!" In the end, I was not chosen to be the school model student, and I did not receive any apology from the teachers' committee. Not only did I feel rejected, but there was a great sense of shame that I could not comprehend.

Self-Parenting to Heal the Wounds

Bringing myself back to the present moment, the heaviness near my heart area did not reduce. I was scanning through my body, going back to my heart area. Not only did I feel the heaviness, I had to breathe consciously. After a while, I started feeling nausea and then threw up. My body then became relaxed. I went back to my Inner Child Visualization and connected back to my eight-year-old self. My adult self told her gently that she did not know how to deal with the situation better. In my mind, my adult self held my eight-year-old self in her arms and said, "It is okay now. I am here with you. You did not get a chance to explain yourself. I hear you; you did not know your books were scribbled in. You were shocked too. Of course, you wanted to be a good role model too. Most importantly, you will not deal with this by yourself. I am standing by you no matter what happens." At that moment, I felt heaviness in my chest (e.g., my breaths were irregular, mixed with short and long breaths, heavy and shallow breaths). I went on and said, "Thank you for staying connected with me. I would also like to acknowledge your resilience and hold this feeling up after all these years. What would be something you would like me to learn from this?"

I could hear my inner voice say, *Others may have doubts about you, but Jenny, you cannot doubt yourself. You need to be the first and last person who believes in you, and you can achieve anything you want in life*. I was touched and moved by this learning that happened within me. My tears were the traces of my shed layers and were released from my inner child's wound. I forged a deeper and closer connection with myself. "Thank you, Jenny, for reminding me about this trust I need to give to myself."

After sitting with myself for a while, I continued to stay connected with my eight-year-old self in this visualization process.

I asked, "Little Jenny, are you ready to follow me and go back to the present moment?" I paused for a while, and continued, "Would you like to go back to where I am now by taking the magic carpet?" My eight-year-old self nodded her head, and we took the magic carpet and came back home. The home within me and the home where I am at that moment, the reality. Slowly, as I focused on my breathing, I brought myself back to where I was sitting in my living room.

Though at the end of this Inner Child Visualization, I was still feeling some heaviness in my chest, I felt a more spacious and expansive space from within. I decided to proceed with a Wu Tao Dance guided meditation on water and fire elements. I was just allowing my body to contain all the emotions I had at that time, and I shed tears again when I heard these words: "Love is all there is. Come home to love." A great sense of release had softened me from inside out. This is a way of the self-healing process and journey.

You may already have your own ways that have helped you and get you back to your center and core. Here is an additional way to get unstuck. Getting to know more about yourself through observation will help you see where and why you get stuck. "Home" is your inner core that gives you strength to stay at your truth, that helps you get back to your core and holds you gently when you are facing difficult times. Most importantly, you need to be willing to get out from your patterns and spirals and keep the change within you.

seven

APPLYING THE CARE METHOD

I used to think that there would be an end or I could retire from being a mother (i.e., it may be as soon as my child turns twenty-one years old, and I can then relinquish my role). When I became a conscious mother, I finally realized that there are always some triggers we will discover as our children grow from milestone to milestone. Even in adult children, we may see our children as "mirrors" that project our inner wounds from time to time. Yes, many parents would agree that once you and I become parents, we are going to be parents until our child parents us back, or we will be parents till the very end of our life journey. We will continue to have breakthroughs and breakdowns throughout. One thing I am very clear about is as long as you have become a conscious parent, you will be aware of your breakthroughs and breakdowns, you will have much courage to face these ups and downs, and you can be very sure that you have the skills to bring yourself back to neutrality and calmness. You will even accept that these ups and downs are just part of life. Surrendering to life leads you to nonresistance of these moments.

Yes, I have discussed in previous chapters about the conflicts Ally and I were having due to online games. In this chapter, we are going to apply the CARE Method to practice alternative ways to support our children in the present moment. I bring this up a few times because it is important for us to get to the core of why we are triggered by certain things that our children do. Using this particular example, how my child triggered my anxiety over online games, I realized this is a learning opportunity to learn about myself and my fear. This is the "pain" that I need to heal to clear the barrier between my child and me, so that I can build deeper relationship with myself through my child. Previously, I saw I was a controlling mother because of my fear that my child might be addicted to online games. Deep down, I was afraid of finding out or admitting I was not a good enough mother for my child; therefore, she could go to online games to seek comfort or relief. I also got us to pay attention to our behavior, emotion, and action at the present moment and make conscious choices about connecting with our children. Furthermore, this trigger continued to resurface, because I had yet to fully learn the lessons I needed to learn. I realized it triggered my old childhood wound of rejection. I was once rejected, and when I interacted with my child, and she did not take my advice to control her time playing online games, similar emotion resurfaced, and I felt rejected by her. My body remembered that rejection; it brought me back straight to that moment during childhood, even though I was not aware of it. After I reconciled with my younger self, also known as my inner child, I can now give myself that compassionate space, and I am no longer blindly or less likely triggered by the rejection. It gives me a sense of relief and I am able to hold that space for my child to learn about her online game habits.

That day, she was playing an online game in her room with her friends. I decided to give her space by not intruding in her room. I texted her using online messaging and asked what time she would end her game. She replied to me once without an answer and did not continue to reply even though she read my messages. My mind was filled with my own stories of how rude she was for not replying to me. While *checking in with myself*, I observed my inner chaos or weather, felt my physiological reaction, and wanted to create a safe space for my child. It was around eleven o'clock at home, it was past bedtime, and I was a little tired. I heard two inner voices in my head: (1) How could my daughter, Ally, not reply to me? (2) If I could overcome what I was experiencing (i.e., emotional reactivity) and trust she could end her online game within half an hour, this could be the greatest gift I could give to Ally and me. When I was listening to the first inner voice, "How could my daughter, Ally, not reply to me?" I could feel I was emotionally charged for being ignored; I wanted to just go into Ally's room and ask her to end the game immediately. I could feel my cheeks were warm, and my heartbeat was pounding faster than usual.

I chose to *attune to Ally's needs*, her need to be trusted, and to have the space to practice self-control by giving her a little reminder. Hence, I inserted a conscious pause and brought back *Calm Jenny*.[1] I decided to explore the second inner voice further. I knocked on her door and asked her to read my messages. She came out and said she was sorry and she did not read my messages even though they were checked as read, and she did not know why. At that moment, I reminded myself to attune to Ally's needs (i.e., to listen to her apology) and choose my role as an observer. I *reconnected with myself and her, I remembered to stay in the present moment*, I sensed my heart beats were going faster, and based on past experiences, I knew if I were to open my mouth right away, I might not have said anything that would be constructive. I did not say anything. At eleven thirty at night, I accepted her apology and asked her to go to bed. I switched off the light in her room and sat in her room for a while. I did not say a word. I watched her at the side and watched my inner chaos. After a while, I went back to my room.

The next morning, after breakfast, we spoke about what had happened the previous night. Each of us got to share our perspective on what happened. She explained that she was not

---

1   Chapter 3 "Album of Different Personalities" Exercise.

aware of my new messages and apologized again. I told her that I would accept her apology for not responding to my messages. I also told her what I learned from this interaction, which was that I needed her to hold herself accountable for following the agreed end time for her to end the online game. I asked what she could do differently, and she said she would remember to put an alarm clock to remind her about the end time. We *expressed our gratitude and celebrated* how we were able to communicate openly and share how we felt and what we could do differently.

During your daily interactions with your child, you can apply a four-step CARE Method and build your Conscious Parenting practice over time.

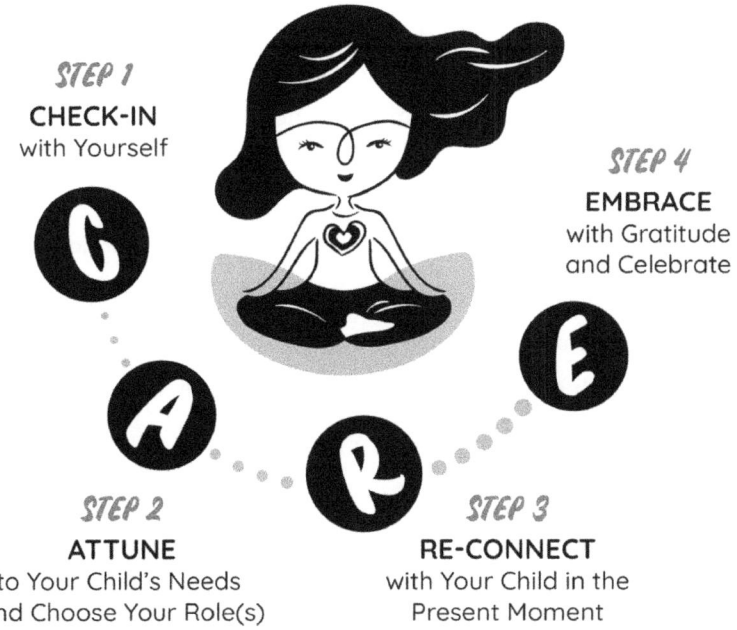

STEP 1
CHECK-IN
with Yourself

STEP 4
EMBRACE
with Gratitude
and Celebrate

STEP 2
ATTUNE
to Your Child's Needs
and Choose Your Role(s)

STEP 3
RE-CONNECT
with Your Child in the
Present Moment

FOUR STEPS TO CARE

Step 1: Check in with Yourself

Stop and check in with yourself, find out what has happened, and listen to your inner self-talk and your child's behaviors and possibly identify your child's needs beyond her behavior. You can become more aware of your current state: emotionally or physically. Do you need to break away from any lacks or negativities before you show up in front of your child? For instance, "I am upset with myself because I have not completed any items on my to-do list. I feel lousy right now!" Pause and be aware of this emotional state, accept and treat yourself like your friend, sit with yourself for a short while, and when you are ready you can connect with your child again, or you can insert your conscious pause and choose not to react to it. Move your attention and awareness from the mind to the heart before interacting with your child.

Step 2: Attune to Your Child's Needs and Choose Your Role(s)

Who do you need to be in order to support your child at the present moment: a friend, a coach, or an observer (mirror)? These are the roles you can choose from depending on your child's need(s). You can choose to be:

- A friend:
  - You can play with your child like a peer/friend of him/her.

- You can apply active listening to your child when he/she is bearing emotional baggage.

- A coach:
  - You can provide guidance to your child when he/she is encountering challenges. You can help him/her to see, or brainstorm the options he/she could have to solve the problem. You can also hold the space for him/her to accept the consequences that come with the option he/she has chosen, and he/she can be responsible to deal with them.
  - You can be your child's emotional coach. After listening to your child with compassion, you can again hold the space for your child to regulate his/her own emotion, or should he/she decide to let his/her emotion out safely, or not to deal with it at that moment. In short, you take care of your own emotional state, which also allows your child to take care of his/her own emotional state without having to deal with yours. This could help ease his/her stress and give him/her space to gather his/her inner resources.
  - You can help your child to see mistakes as learning opportunities and guide him/her to be responsible for every decision made.
  - Should your child face conflicts, you can coach your child to apply negotiation skills to achieve win–win solutions.

- Over time, as you master the CARE method, you can start thinking of supporting your child as a coach by getting them to build new skills (e.g., scheduling their daily routines, establishing quality friendships, etc.)

- An observer:
  - You can reflect your child's strengths back to him/her like a mirror.
  - You can value positive reinforcement such as words of affirmation and specific praise, and apply it to help your child to build self-confidence and resilience.
  - You can remind your child of his/her old patterns/habits, your family rules, boundaries, lessons learned, etc. during neutral time when you and your child are calm.

Step 3: Reconnect with Your Child in the Present Moment

Apply the breathing technique and bring yourself to the present moment. For parents who are still strengthening your mindfulness muscle, you may choose alternative ways such as touching your bracelet or pendant, and bring yourself back to the here and now. Realign with your commitment when practicing Conscious Parenting from the place of love. When you are reconnecting with your child, you choose to be 100 percent present, not in the past or future, because that will create fear or control, which will be the hindrance between your heart-to-heart connection. In the present moment, think about what you and your child need to learn from where you are. Furthermore, as you bring yourself back to the present moment, you have space to reconnect with who you truly are. From this place of love, you can stay rooted and centered to support your child.

Step 4: Embrace with Gratitude and Celebrate

You can embrace what happened with your gratitude for this given learning opportunity, as well as celebrate the success of how both of you are able to connect with one another, and overcome the hurdles or patterns that may have hindered both of your growth and connection. You can observe your thoughts and consciously choose your words and actions before saying out loud or taking action that you may regret later. Not to forget, how you talk to your child(ren) is most likely how you talk to yourself (i.e., your internal self-talk).

APPLICATION OF THE CARE METHOD

Apply the CARE Method using the incident (i.e., my child's online game habits and not replying my texts) as example:

Step 1: Check in with Yourself

Observe your inner weather, or internal self-talks, as well as the following states:

Are both you and your child feeling safe where you are?

How is your physical well-being? Are you and your child tired?

While physiological reactions, such as racing heartbeats, shallow breathing, tensed muscles, facial muscle responses, body temperature, etc., sit in the physical body, they are what you experience when your emotion is triggered, e.g., when one is angry, he or she may experience muscle tension, racing heartbeats, increased breathing rates, flushed face due to increased blood flow, etc.

Step 2: Attune to Your Child's Needs, and Choose Your Role(S), e.g., Friend, Coach, Observer

Attune to your child's need(s) at the moment, e.g., to be given space and opportunity to learn self-control and manage her screen time. You can first choose to be the observer and remind her the agreement on screen time. As time goes by, you may consider the choice to play another alternative role if your child is lacking self-control skills. You may switch to your coach hat and support her to end the screen time on her own.

Step 3: Reconnect with Your Child in the Present Moment

Be mindful about your negative self-talk that might be driven out of your fear. Listen to your inner dialogue.

You could observe your thoughts, choose your words and actions before saying them out loud or taking action. Reconnect with your truth and stay rooted to show up for your child.

(Note: How you talk to your child(ren) is most likely how you talk to yourself.)

Step 4: Embrace with Gratitude and Celebrate

You can embrace what happened and release your ego, or "I get to be right!" You can also express gratitude toward your child and acknowledge an area she has done well, area(s) she can improve, and/or area(s) she can do differently next time.

Kerry's Story: What Is Wrong with Me?

The other day, Kelly brought her son to a class that both agreed upon to take up. She was delighted and she even imagined he would put on a happy face during the class. However, when they reached there, Kelly's son was not open to joining the class, and she found it really hard on her after all the research and preparation. She lost her cool. In Kelly's mind, her son would put on a happy smile, and when the reality did not match what she imagined, she was devastated and disappointed.

Let us see how it would look like if Kerry applied the CARE Method to soothe her frustration when her son was not showing interest in the activities she planned wholeheartedly for.

Step 1: Check in with Yourself

Kerry could observe her inner voice and feel her physiological reaction. At the same time, she could observe her child.

Kerry could check with her inner weather. She might realize she was frustrated, and started feeling impatient. Her palms might get sweaty, and her heart could pound faster.

She could insert a conscious pause here, and listen to her inner voices:

Voice 1: *I am so frustrated right now, I feel like letting this frustration out, and leaving this place immediately. Why is my son not appreciating my effort? I have spent so much time looking up this lesson that I have been thinking this will be fun for him, he has to grab this precious opportunity to play with other children.*

Voice 2: *What can I learn from this? I can feel my not-good-enough self just triggered. I know this ego self. Not-good-enough self, you can stand aside now, I need space to regulate my frustration first.*

As she could practice the breathing technique, this would help her have space to pay attention to her son. She could observe her son was standing at one corner, not looking as excited as she imagined he would be.

Step 2: Attune to Your Child's Needs, and Choose Your Role(s), e.g., Friend, Coach, Observer

Kerry might decide to go near him, and hold his hand. "How are you feeling?" She could ask, "Would you like to stay a little longer and observe the children first? Mummy will be here with you." Kerry could stay by her son's side, and both of them could observe a little longer.

Step 3: Reconnect with Your Child in the Present Moment

Be aware that your judgmental voices might reappear, empty them. Tell yourself you got this.

Kerry could go to her child's eye-level, and ask him gently, "Would you like to join the group?" Kerry could read her son's body language and his tone of voice before she could decide her next steps, for instance, she could let her son choose to either stay or leave the place.

(Note: How you talk to your child(ren) is most likely how you talk to yourself.)

Step 4: Embrace with Gratitude and Celebrate

Kerry could embrace what happened, and release her egoic self that her son had to go along with her plan; she imagined he would enjoy this activity.

Kerry could express gratitude toward this learning opportunity because she finally realized her son did not enjoy this type of activity. She could embrace the imperfection of how it turned out. At the same time, she could let her son know what she found out about him, mirrored back to her son. And yet to let her son know what she would do differently next time, e.g., to plan the activity together.

The key that would truly help Kerry here is to apply the CARE Method, so that she could be truly present at the activity venue and support her child is to be a mindful observer of herself. At that point, when her expectation of her child did not match the behavior exhibited by her real child, she could be emotionally hijacked by unconscious old patterns of her past. (Kerry could revisit the source of pain that triggered her at a later time.) When she is emotionally hijacked, she might not be able to activate the CARE Method. She would need to tap on her deep breathing, her bracelet, her pendant, or her own personalized item to help her stay in the present moment and be grounded in her body.

Lu's Story: My Teenager Would Not Talk to Me

Lu's daughter turned fourteen and buried herself in computer games day and night. She skipped school every now and then, when all students were required to go back to school after the outbreak of COVID-19 was stabilized.

Lu was away and worked in a different city to make a living for the betterment of the family. Lu's daughter was taken care of by her grandparents and father since she was in preschool. At home, her grandparents and father were physically present; however, they were not able to provide empathy or emotional support to the child. Lu stayed in touch with her daughter via phone calls and visited the hometown during public holidays.

Lu went back home for a visit when she found out her daughter had skipped school. It was a short stay. Lu wanted to see some change in her daughter immediately and decided to snatch and confiscate the phone from her. Their relationship worsened by this; after Lu returned to work, her daughter refused to pick up her phone call and decided to shut down their communication.

Apply the CARE Method using the previous example: "My Teenager Would Not Talk to Me."

Step 1: Check in with Yourself

Lu could observe and check in with her mind and body (e.g., her inner weather, thoughts, emotions, physiological reactions, etc.).

How was she feeling? How was her child feeling? Were both of them safe, or would they be judged?

How was her physical well-being? Were both of them tired? If yes, she could find another time or make them both feel comfortable and relaxed.

She could observe her inner chaos and feel her physiological reaction. Was her heartbeat racing faster and faster? How could she help herself to calm down (e.g., taking deep breaths)?

Step 2: Attune to Your Child's Needs and Choose Your Role(s) (e.g., Friend, Coach, Observer)

Her child wanted to play online games and did not want to go to school. Lu was very worried. She could first acknowledge her own anxiety having to hear that her child did not want to attend school anymore. Once she was able to observe what happened and not go straight to her guilt (e.g., I did not do well as a mother) or shame (e.g., I am a bad mother) to react, she could then continue to meet her child where she was. She could attune to her child's need(s) by sharing with her child, "I know it may be hard for you these days; you could not talk to me as I have been away for work. These days, online games seem to be your best friends and your go-to playmate. However, I am back now. If you are open to chatting, I want to be your listening ear. Is it a good time to chat?" She had decided to be her friend at this moment. If her child was open to chat, Lu could also find the right time to share how worried she was when she heard that her child decided not to go to school. She could ask her daughter what might have bothered her and shared with her daughter her own observations on how much she enjoyed school in the past. If her child was not ready to share, she could just invite her child to play or do things together, and be ready to accept that her daughter would not reply or do anything she suggested.

Step 3: Reconnect with Your Child in the Present Moment

During the conversation, Lu would be her inner observer of her own self-talk. She could acknowledge internally that those dialogues were driven by fear or love. She would have to choose to stay rooted for both herself and her daughter, and not easily distracted by her own negativity or criticism, but to hold the space for herself and her child.

She could repeat and paraphrase what her child said, and let her child know she was fully attentive to her, and time spent together was precious and important.

Step 4: Embrace with Gratitude and Celebrate

Lu could embrace what happened and release her controlling mode because of her fear or her righteousness (e.g., "I get to be right! I am always right because I am your mother!") Her ultimate goal might be asking her child to go back to school. However, depending where this conversation would lead them, if it was premature, she could end the conversation on a lighter note and express gratitude toward her child for being so open to sharing, and let her child know how much she felt for her, and everything would turn out all right, and she would be there for her. Lu could also ask her child to have more chat sessions when she was home.

As Lu was away too long and too frequently, she would need to be more patient, to give space to her child, so that her child could feel that she was honored as a fourteen-year-old. Lu could also acknowledge and embrace her anxiety that came from her past, i.e., she had been through a lot on her own. Since her youth, she had been telling herself to get out of the small town and she was very determined to want to change her life and break the cycle of poverty. One of her wishes would be seeing her daughter have a better life than she had. She could celebrate her love for, and with, her daughter. Though anxious, she was committed to be there for her daughter, provided guidance and safety net, so that her daughter could get clarity moving forward.

Conscious Self-Parenting and Reflection

Try it out: practice the CARE Method and connect with your child from heart to heart. You can recall a past interaction with your child, reflect and be guided with the CARE Method, and explore alternative ways you can interact with your child next time.

Step #	CARE Method	What You Can Do
Step 1	Check in with yourself.	
Step 2	Attune to your child's needs and choose your role(s) (e.g., friend, coach, observer).	
Step 3	Reconnect with your child in the present moment.	
Step 4	Embrace with gratitude and celebrate.	

In order to apply the CARE Method effectively, you must first care for yourself, know where you are, and know at what state you are in before you connect and attune to your child's needs. Depending on your state and balance with your child's needs, you can decide whether you are going to play the roles as a friend, as a coach, or as an observer to reflect your child's strengths and/ or weaknesses. Meet your child where he or she is, reconnect with yourself and your child in the present moment, embrace what happens outside of both of you, be grateful for the learning opportunity, and celebrate what both of you did well.

Here are some positive side effects of applying the CARE Method and being a conscious parent. I show up as who I am and express my true feelings and honest thinking in the present moment. This means I allow myself to be vulnerable to admit my mistakes and human errors, I apologize to my child sincerely, and I face my imperfection. With my authentic parenting, my child is given invisible permission to share her true feelings and honest thinking without hiding or covering up her authentic self. This deep and genuine connection between us forges trust and mutual respect.

From time to time, my child or I may say to the other, "I know what you are going to say or do..." by observing the other through facial cues, eye contact, body language, or without finishing what we are saying. At times, we may also receive some signals to not say a word. This freedom to express ourselves helps us to build healthy relationships and to request an apology when we feel hurt by the judgment of the other.

Little by little, Ally is learning and practicing to form healthy relationships with herself, her peers, and people around her. When she was eleven, there were times when she was feeling down, sad, and lonely because her friends were not actively engaged with her, or they were not keeping their word when they agreed to play online games with her. She keeps showing up as who she truly is when she is with her friends. She is twelve now; she is having fun with her friends over online games, visiting their houses, and exchanging messages that bring her laughter most of the time. There are still times where she feels frustrated, disappointed, and bored when her friends are not responding to her the way she wishes they would.

A few things I observe she does well: she communicates straight with her friends about her likes and dislikes, respects their boundaries, and at the same time, is highly aware of her own loose boundaries, which she does not mind. However, when need be, she will still say no to her friends. This also helps her to build more trusting relationships with her besties. There are still many challenges and learning opportunities that lie ahead of her as she is entering secondary school. While I trust that she can tap on her inner strengths and resources to practice and overcome these challenges, she is highly aware of my unwavering commitment to be there for her when she needs me to be her sturdy "cotton tree" to provide support, advice, and/or comfort.

As a conscious mother and coach, I am breaking old patterns started from my parents' parents' parents and on and on:

our ancestors. I am working toward unchaining myself from repeating the patterns through healing. In other words, as my pain from childhood wounds is being reduced through healing, I am also reducing the pain of my child, which she may have experienced when she was younger or along her growing-up journey. If not, I am helping her to make sense of her experiences, or bringing her different perspectives when she is interpreting these experiences. Not only that, I am also observing her growth using my own Ever-Evolving Self & Continuous Self-Growth as guidelines. Ally is usually staying at *Self-Trust* (Stage 2 from Chapter 3—The Ever-Evolving Self & Continuous Self-Growth) as her default. From a recent interaction she had with her friend, I notice she is given opportunities to practice Self-Compassion (Stage 3) and Self-Resiliency (Stage 4). Recently, she has come to me and shared her frustration about her interaction with her friend. She has caught herself feeling guilty because she did not spend enough time with her friend. With compassion, she is committed to spending more time and making up to her friend. Unfortunately, her friend does not respond positively to her proposal to go for an outing together. She feels disappointed. However, because she is aware of her guilt, and she treasures this friendship very much, she counter-proposes an alternative date and time after an hour of disappointment. I reflect these strengths she displayed from this incident to her as an observer; bit by bit, this can help her recall her strengths and retrieve her inner resources when she needs it.

Practice the CARE Method to support your child's growth. Can you see how you are growing together with your child(ren) as you practice it?

CONCLUSION

While writing this book, I observed my own internal struggle to follow my writing plan. I would get stuck and lose focus on why I was writing this book. It is easy to see this as backsliding in my awakening journey, my progress toward my true self. However, the fact that I am able to *observe and be aware of* where I am and what emotional states I am in is itself proof of my progress. I now have the power to bring myself back on track, follow my life purpose, and attend to the people who are important in my life—like you, reader. In fact, the way we live life is cycling in a pattern; we are patterns living in a pattern. Breaking through some of these old patterns from time to time seems inevitable; however, as we are unchaining ourselves or breaking through one cycle of patterns after another, we are progressing to get closer to knowing ourselves better, and evolving to connect with our higher purpose in life, and possibly reaching self-transcendence stage, the *N stage* described in Chapter 3—Unchaining Yourself from Old Patterns, and Progressing toward Continuous Self-Growth.

Unchaining Yourself from Old Patterns and Progressing toward Continuous Self-Growth

Browsing through my journals, I relived my recorded rebirth into my true self. I am sure there were many more rebirths that I did not get to pen down, but I noted my external changes to validate my achievements, and I ridiculed myself for what I had not achieved. I would feel sad for a few days when my parents commented how my other siblings or their friends' children were doing better than me, even in my early thirties. I was still struggling to meet their expectations of me and longing to make them proud of me.

I NO LONGER NEED TO PROVE MYSELF

In these recent years, along my personal growth journey, I have been reminding myself to cherish my being, and letting go of trying too hard to prove that "I am worth it." I am living in the present moment and embracing "anything can happen any time," and giving myself space to make friends with uncertainties.

While moving toward cocreating my life with people and things around me, I know I will occasionally slow myself down, occasionally doubt myself, occasionally hesitate—at times, even get lost for a moment. However, I also know I can always find my "North Star," go back on track, and move toward my life goals again. You just read my awakened journey: how I regained my true self, rediscovered the person I was born to be, and continue to discover my new possibilities in myself. There is always a new beginning to every learning we attain. I hope my Unchained-through-Self-Parenting process can give you alternative perspectives to learn about yourself, to get curious to discover your authentic truth, and to be open-minded to ask yourself about how your life can be.

Are you ready to be a conscious observer of life? While pursuing external successes, can you see that you are shedding skin chronologically (age) from the outside? Can you see that your life keeps diminishing?

Let us pause and ask ourselves, since life keeps diminishing in every second, what are the things truly worth collecting and pursuing in life?

When we choose to be a traveler of our own life journey and learn to allow the process of shedding (-) layers of our ego from the inside, we get to uncover our true self from within. From this place, we gain clarity of who it is we truly are, and we grow (+) our wisdom, experience, and strength.

What is truly worth collecting and growing in life? Collecting things from outside to prove your worth? Or growing your inner knowing that you are already worthy, and collecting your strength from within and living the life you want? Having gone through unchaining your old patterns through parenting or self-parenting, I hope you realize that you have the freedom to choose to live your life the way you want it to be.

MY UNCHAINED-THROUGH-
SELF-PARENTING PROCESS

	Healing Inner	Conscious
Awareness	Wound	Observation

Inner Being	**SPHERIC Daily Practice**	**Dancing with Life**

ATTITUDE
THE INTEGRATION OF THINK/FEEL/DO

- **Awareness:** You can become aware that your true self was trapped from within; it feels like your other self is waiting to be "unchained" or "awakened." Or you do not enjoy the outside you or your false self. Or you feel that it is not the real you.

- **Healing Inner Wounds:** You realize there are inner wounds that keep you away from your true self, or you create walls or barriers that stop you from reaching your inner truth or true self. There are many approaches and methods that can be used to heal your wounds and connect with your true self. Some of my favorite ones are conscious coaching and Compassionate Inquiry.

- **Conscious Observation:** Through mindfulness, you can observe your thoughts, feelings, and sensations without reacting or judging, and stay in the present moment. As soon as you observe your breaths drifting away from your philtrum, you can just simply observe them, and return to your breaths again. With this conscious observation of yourself, you can check in with yourself, connect with your internal self-talks, and observe your being at the present moment. Some questions you may have in your inner dialogues are: What do I think? How do I feel? What do I do next? When required, you may make good choices, so that you can gain the outcomes you want in life or build a close and loving relationship with your child.

• **Inner Being:** Breathing meditation and mindfulness strengthen your mental muscle and self-regulation to be a strong inner world observer. During your daily practice, you are connecting with your inner being through your mind and body by doing introspective activities, such as Wu Tao Dance Therapy, meditation, etc. Honoring your inner being is similar to honoring your existence without asking to do better or do more, or proving your worth. Your presence on this planet in itself is a beauty.

• **SPHERIC Daily Practice:** With SPHERIC, you have the essential elements (e.g., daily intention setting at your fingertips to decide where you are at the present moment) and what you need to get to where you want to lead your inner state toward achieving your goals or executing an action plan.

- **Dancing with Life:** As you are having so much clarity living your life, you can wake up with gratitude each morning to move toward your life goals one step at a time. You may apply the CARE Method, so that you can better support your child in the present moment. You can also notice your fear and understand where it comes from, and appreciate its intention to protect you from being hurt, especially emotionally. As you can embrace your fear more, you can find your courage to choose different actions and move on. At the end of the day, you are grateful for things that happen to you or do not happen to you. Most importantly, use a natural gesture to hug yourself with love and compassion, or close your eyes with a little smile and say to yourself silently, "Thank you for everything, (you)!"

Here I am, paraphrasing from Eckhart Tolle from one live teaching,

The being of every human aligns with evolving consciousness; it gives in the state of absolute presence. This presence can be contagious, and it affects many many others, the transmission of presence in some miraculous way, and it manifests a better world or an emanation of kindness.[1]

---

1   Tolle, "Eckhart Tolle Special Live Teaching."

According to A.H. Almaas in his Diamond Heart Series, the being is the essence of who you are without boundaries, without definition, just openness. When you experience essence, there will be space, openness, and inner spaciousness. The being is in the sense that it is an existence. Essence is the truth of your very presence, the authentic presence of your being, the purity of your consciousness and awareness. It is the true nature of who you are, your true self, and it has nothing to do with your personality, your emotions, your ideas, your self-concept, your self-image, your accomplishments, your preferences, your likes and dislikes, your relationships. Your beingness is always pure, always present, always whole and complete.[2] While your mind may tell you that you ought to become a better person, your heart knows that the real work lies in connecting with your truth. Your priority is to discover your essence and manifest your authentic self, the real you, into this world.

JOIN OUR COMMUNITY

Are you ready to discover your truth from within, and be courageous to awaken your aliveness? Having read this book, I hope you see the light and possibilities of taking it on for you and your loved ones.

For parents who want to create extraordinary relationships with yourself and your children, you want to remember that

---

2   The Diamond Approach, "Quotes about Essence."

enjoying your parenting journey is a conscious choice. We are a bunch of parents who dare to ask for more, and curious about what we are made of, and not afraid to keep trying until we uncover our authentic truth by awakening our true self. Why do we work so hard to get there? Because we know if we do not, we may lose the opportunity to enjoy and experience the beauty of the "sunrise" or "sunset" moments within our own family life. In other words, the ups and downs in life as a family. We can cherish every mistake made, or every lesson learned, because we know this is another precious opportunity for us to grow. We are not afraid of challenges, as we know we have our inner strengths to deal with any challenges.

Come and join us; together we will keep you energized and keep you going until you get there. Many of us come from different walks of life and places around the globe and we get connected as we share the same parental goals. We are there for each other when we are having tough times coping with life, and many of us have turned into lifelong friends. Conscious Parenting and conscious living is a lifelong journey. Meet us here at Conscious Parents for Life: *facebook.com/groups/Conscious ParentsforLife.*

I applaud you for being curiously interested in embarking on this journey to becoming a conscious parent and conscious individual.

Thank you for contributing to the progress of social change. I look forward to seeing you joining my community. I would also love to connect with you via email or social media and hear your journey and sharing. Together, we are working toward "healing humanity via parenting, one child at a time."

I am so grateful to be able to reconnect with my true self in this lifetime. I got to connect with my essence and express it in different ways, including writing this book to my life experiences of this self-awakening journey. If you are hesitating in embarking on this self-discovery journey, I hope this book gives you some courage to set off. When you get to "meet" and connect with your authentic self, I want to welcome you, and say, "Hi, Me! Yes! I am found, and let us dance through life together! Thank you for not giving up on me!" Be courageous to face yourself, the part of you that you love, the part of you that you do not want to acknowledge. When you are able to embrace all of you, that is where you start saying, "I am worthy, and I am worthy to have a fulfilling life. I deserve better than this (where you are at the present moment)."

Lastly, I would like to end this book with a quote from John Maxwell:

> I often teach that we have two great tasks in life: to find ourselves and to lose ourselves. Ultimately, I believe we find ourselves by discovering our *why*. We lose ourselves while traveling the path of significance by putting others first... When I die, I cannot take with me what I have, but I can live in others by what I gave.[3]

---

3   Maxwell, *The Power of Significance*, 8.

What is more precious to know is that you and I can live with our children by what we can give them through daily deposits of our true love into their lives. This true love flows out naturally through the continuous evolution of our truth.

Be courageous to seek for your truth. I wish for you to find your life purpose and enjoy the beautiful journey of life.

TOOLS & RESOURCES

- R. Emmons, "10 Ways to Become More Grateful: Robert Emmons Offers Everyday Tips for Living A Life Of Gratitude," *The Greater Good Science Center at the University of California, Berkeley*, https://greatergood.berkeley.edu/article/item/ten_ways_to_become_more_grateful1/
- Janet Philbin, *Show Up for Yourself: A Guide to Inner Growth and Awareness*.
- D. Osman, "Eye Accessing Cues & Representational Systems—What They Mean & How to Use Them," *Medium*, https://medium.com/@dina.osman/eye-accessing-cues-representational-systems-what-they-mean-how-to-use-them-45097cc7b50a.
- Resources of self-compassion exercises by Dr. Kristin Neff. Retrieved from https://self-compassion.org/resources-2.

- S. Shapiro, *Good Morning, I Love You: Mindfulness and Self-compassion Practices to Rewire Your Brain for Calm, Clarity, and Joy*.
- Self-compassion exercise by Jamie Lynn: http://www.whollymindful.com/videos-and-lessons.html.

MY GO-TO WISDOM TEACHERS

- Dr Shefali Tsabary YouTube videos: https://www.youtube.com/channel/UCKzsU94h-PkLBiF5xH0-SjQ
- Gary Zukav YouTube videos: https://www.youtube.com/user/theseatofthesoul/videos
- Eckhart Tolle YouTube videos: https://www.youtube.com/c/EckhartTolle/featured
- Dr. Gabor Maté YouTube videos: https://www.youtube.com/channel/UCsRF06lSFA8zV9L8_x9jzIA
- Dr. Dan Siegel YouTube videos: https://www.youtube.com/user/mindsightinstitute/featured
- Thích Nhất Hạnh's 4 Mantras YouTube video: https://youtu.be/UEUxFNkISnU
  - "Darling, I'm here for you."
  - "Darling, I know you are there."

- "Darling, I know you suffer, that is why I am here for you."
- "Darling, I suffer, I try my best to practice, please help me."

BIBLIOGRAPHY

INTRODUCTION

APA Dictionary of Psychology, s.v., "intrapersonal intelligence." Accessed April 17, 2023. https://dictionary.apa.org/intrapersonal-intelligence.

Arakelyan, Hayk S. "False Omniscient Personality Disorder (True Self and False Self)." September 2020. https://www.researchgate.net/publication/344160960_False_Omniscient_Personality_Disorder_True_self_and_false_self.

Kempton, Beth. *Wabi Sabi: Japanese Wisdom for a Perfectly Imperfect Life*. New York: Harper Design, 2018.

Lynch, Matthew. "Intrapersonal Intelligence: Everything You Need to Know." The Tech Edvocate, October 30, 2022. https://www.thetechedvocate.org/intrapersonal-intelligence-everything-you-need-to-know/.

CHAPTER 1

Alfaya, Cristiane Ajnamei dos Santos. "Response to the Editorial 'Psycho-Emotional Care in a Neonatal Unit During the COVID-19 Pandemic." *Revista Paulista de Pediatria* 40 (2022). https://doi.org/10.1590/1984-0462/2022/40/2020457.

Grossberg, Bella. "Let Your Inner Child Dance." In *Dance Therapy Collections* 2, edited by Jane Guthrie, Elizabeth Loughlin, and Diane Albiston, 50–53. Australia: DTAA, 1999.

Hạnh, Thích Nhất. *Reconciliation: Healing the Inner Child.* Berkeley, CA: Parallax Press, 2006.

McKeever, Niall. "True or False: Winnicott's Notions of Self." *The Weekend University*, April 3, 2020. https://theweekenduniversity.com/true-or-false-winnicotts-notions-of-self/.

Redden, Francesca. "Guided Inner Child Visualisation." 2017. Audio file. SoundCloud. 27:50. https://soundcloud.com/francescaredden/guided-inner-child-visualisation?utm_source=clipboard&utm_medium=text&utm_campaign=social_sharing.

Tolle, Eckhart. "Eckhart Tolle Special Live Teaching | Conscious Manifestation." Eckhart Tolle. June 20, 2020. YouTube video. 1:23:40. https://www.youtube.com/watch?v=8G46F9ye204.

Whitfield, Charles L. Healing the Child Within: Discovery and Recovery for Adult Children of Dysfunctional Families. Deerfield Beach, FL: Health Communications, 1987.

Winnicott, D. W. "Ego Distortion in Terms of True and False Self (1960)." In The Maturational Processes and the Facilitating Environment. New York: International Universities Press, 1965. https://www.sas.upenn.edu/~cavitch/pdf-library/Winnicott_EgoDistortion.pdf.

CHAPTER 2

Agness, Lindsey. *Change Your Business with NLP: Powerful Tools to Improve Your Organisation's Performance and Get Results.* Chichester, UK: Capstone Publishing, 2010.

American Dance Therapy Association. "What is Dance/Movement Therapy?" Accessed April 17, 2023. https://adta.memberclicks.net/what-is-dancemovement-therapy.

Campbell, Ali. *NLP Made Easy: How to Use Neuro-Linguistic Programming to Change Your Life.* Carlsbad, CA: Hay House, 2018.

Cherry, Kendra. "How Meditation Impacts Your Mind and Body." Verywell Mind. Last modified April 11, 2023. https://www.verywellmind.com/what-is-meditation-2795927.

Clinical Practice Guideline for the Treatment of Posttraumatic Stress Disorder. "What is Psychotherapy?" APA.org. Last modified July 31, 2017. https://www.apa.org/ptsd-guideline/patients-and-families/psychotherapy.

Compassionate Inquiry. "The Approach." Accessed April 17, 2023. https://compassionateinquiry.com/the-approach/.

Emmons, Robert. "How Gratitude Can Help You Through Hard Times." *Greater Good Magazine*, May 13, 2013. https://greatergood.berkeley.edu/article/item/how_gratitude_can_help_you_through_hard_times. Reprinted with permission.

Golden, Bernard. "Mindfulness Meditation and Psychotherapy." *Psychology Today*, February 3, 2019. https://www.psychologytoday.com/sg/blog/overcoming-destructive-anger/201902/mindfulness-meditation-and-psychotherapy.

GoodTherapy. "Journal Therapy." Last modified March 8, 2016. https://www.goodtherapy.org/learn-about-therapy/types/journal-therapy.

Kabat-Zinn, Jon. *Wherever You Go, There You Are: Mindfulness Meditation in Everyday Life.* New York: Hyperion, 1994.

Greater Good Magazine. "What Is Mindfulness?" Accessed April
18, 2023. https://greatergood.berkeley.edu/topic/mindfulness/
definition.

Karkou, Vicky, Supritha Aithal, Ania Zubala, and Bonnie
Meekums. "Effectiveness of Dance Movement Therapy in the
Treatment of Adults with Depression: A Systematic Review
with Meta-Analyses." *Frontiers in Psychology* 10 (May 2019).
https://doi.org/10.3389/fpsyg.2019.00936.

Kennedy, Terry Reis. "Dalai Lama on Generating the Mind for
Enlightenment." Central Tibetan Administration. June 21,
2017. https://tibet.net/dalai-lama-on-generating-the-mind-
for-enlightenment/.

Miller, Alice. *The Body Never Lies: The Lingering Effects of Hurtful
Parenting.* Translated by Andrew Jenkins. New York: W. W.
Norton & Company, 2005.

O'Connor, Joseph, and John Seymour. *Introducing NLP:
Psychological Skills for Understanding and Influencing People.*
London: Thorsons, 1993.

Winfrey, Oprah. "Oprah Talks to Thích Nhất Hạnh." Oprah.com.
March 2010. https://www.oprah.com/spirit/oprah-talks-to-
thich-nhat-hanh/all.

Petrovici, Amalia Mihaela. "Effective Methods of Learning
and Teaching: A Sensory Approach." *Procedia—Social and
Behavioral Sciences* 93 (October 2013): 146–50. https://doi.
org/10.1016/j.sbspro.2013.09.168.

Prasad, Raghavendra. "Rubber Tapping Machine." *International
Research Journal of Engineering and Technology* 7, no. 6 (June
2020): 1235–38. https://www.irjet.net/archives/V7/i6/IRJET-
V7I6230.pdf.

Schultz, Joshua. "5 Differences between Mindfulness and
Meditation." PositivePsychology.com. July 24, 2020. https://

positivepsychology.com/differences-between-mindfulness-meditation.

Shapiro, Shauna L., Linda E. Carlson, John A. Astin, and Benedict Freedman. "Mechanisms of Mindfulness." Journal of Clinical Psychology 62, no. 3 (March 2006): 373–86. https://doi.org/10.1002/jclp.20237. Reprinted with permission.

Siegel, Dan. "What Makes a Healthy Mind." October 6, 2009. In Sounds True: Insights at the Edge. Podcast. 1:08:41. https://www.resources.soundstrue.com/podcast/what-makes-a-healthy-mind.

Sunnataram Forest Monastery. "Mindfulness and Vipassana Meditation." 2015. https://www.sunnataram.org/dhamma-teachings/summary-teachings-2015/mindfulness-and-vipassana-meditation.

Tiret, Holly. "The Benefits Art Therapy Can Have on Mental and Physical Health." Michigan State University. May 25, 2017. https://www.canr.msu.edu/news/the_benefits_art_therapy_can_have_on_mental_and_physical_health.

Tolle, Eckhart. "Eckhart Tolle Special Live Teaching | Conscious Manifestation." Eckhart Tolle. June 20, 2020. YouTube video. 1:23:40. https://www.youtube.com/watch?v=8G46F9ye2o4.

Tsabary, Shefali. The Conscious Parent: Transforming Ourselves, Empowering Our Children. Vancouver: Namaste Publishing, 2010.

Walsh, R., and Shapiro, S. L. "The Meeting of Meditative Disciplines and Western Psychology: A Mutually Enriching Dialogue." American Psychologist 61, no. 3 (2006): 227–39. https://psycnet.apa.org/doi/10.1037/0003-066X.61.3.227. Copyright © 2006, American Psychological Association. Reproduced with permission.

WebMD Editorial Contributors. "Mental Health and Hypnosis." WebMD. September 14, 2021. https://www.webmd.com/mental-health/mental-health-hypnotherapy.

CHAPTER 3

Chapman, Gary, and Ross Campbell. *The 5 Love Languages of Children: The Secret to Loving Children Effectively.* Chicago: Northfield Publishing, 1997.

Cuncic, Arlin. "What to Know about Logotherapy." Verywell Mind. Last modified March 31, 2023. https://www.verywellmind.com/an-overview-of-victor-frankl-s-logotherapy-4159308.

Curry, Caledonia. "My Mother's Addiction Comes from Pain." CNN, February 5, 2014. https://edition.cnn.com/2014/02/05/opinion/curry-addiction-and-pain/index.html.

Iyengar, Udita, Sohye Kim, Sheila Martinez, Peter Fonagy, and Lane Strathearn. "Unresolved Trauma in Mothers: Intergenerational Effects and the Role of Reorganization." *Frontiers in Psychology* 5 (September 2014). https://doi.org/10.3389/fpsyg.2014.00966.

Jensen, Sarah K. G., Vincent Sezibera, Shauna M. Murray, Robert T. Brennan, and Theresa S. Betancourt. "Intergenerational Impacts of Trauma and Hardship through Parenting." *Journal of Child Psychology and Psychiatry* 62, no. 8 (August 2021): 989–99. https://doi.org/10.1111/jcpp.13359.

Lula, Suzi. *The Motherhood Evolution: How Thriving Mothers Raise Thriving Children.* Finn-Phyllis Press, 2016.

Maslow, Abraham H. *The Farther Reaches of Human Nature.* New York: The Viking Press, 1971.

Myss, Caroline. *Why People Don't Heal and How They Can.* New York: Harmony Books, 1997.

Siler, Shaunna, Tami Boreman, and Betty Ferrell. "Pain and Suffering." *Seminars in Oncology Nursing* 35, no. 3 (June 2019): 310–14. https://doi.org/10.1016/j.soncn.2019.04.013.

Te Ara: The Encyclopedia of New Zealand, s.v., "the koru." Accessed April 17, 2023. https://teara.govt.nz/en/photograph/2422/the-koru#.

University of New Mexico. "Food for Thought: Physical vs. Emotional Hunger—What Are You Really Hungry For?" University of New Mexico Human Resources. April 27, 2022. https://hr.unm.edu/articles/newsletter/physical-vs-emotional-hunger-what-are-you-really-hungry.

Wong, Paul T. P. "Meaning-Seeking, Self-Transcendence, and Well-Being." In *Logotherapy and Existential Analysis: Proceedings of the Viktor Frankl Institute Vienna*, edited by Alexander Batthyány. Vol. 1. New York: Springer, 2016. https://doi.org/10.1007/978-3-319-29424-7_27.

CHAPTER 4

Greater Good Magazine. "What Is Mindfulness?" Accessed April 18, 2023. https://greatergood.berkeley.edu/topic/mindfulness/definition.

Krisch, Joshua A. "The Five Stages of Self-Awareness Explain What Babies See in the Mirror." Fatherly. Last modified March 23, 2023. https://www.fatherly.com/health/children-five-stages-self-awareness-mirror-tests.

Maté, Gabor. "Dr. Gabor Maté on Childhood Trauma, the Real Cause of Anxiety, Our 'Insane' Culture and Ayahuasca." HumanWindow. June 14, 2019. YouTube video. 28:40. https://www.youtube.com/watch?v=e7pVoIPWUlI.

Newman, Kira M. "Can Mindfulness Help You Be More Authentic?" *Greater Good Magazine*, October 31, 2016. https://greatergood.berkeley.edu/article/item/can_mindfulness_help_you_be_more_authentic.

Pratt, Cathy, and Melissa Dubie. "Observing Behavior Using A-B-C Data." Indiana Resource Center for Autism, Indiana University Bloomington. 2022. https://www.iidc.indiana.edu/irca/articles/observing-behavior-using-a-b-c-data.html.

Su, Edgar. "Bags Packed, Malaysians Stream into Singapore ahead of Coronavirus Travel Ban." Reuters. March 17, 2020. https://www.reuters.com/article/us-health-coronavirus-singapore-workers-idCAKBN2142E2.

Tan, Chade-Meng. *Search Inside Yourself: The Unexpected Path to Achieving Success, Happiness (and World Peace)*. New York: HarperOne, 2012.

Tolle, Eckhart. *A New Earth: Awakening to Your Life's Purpose*. New York: Dutton, 2005.

CHAPTER 5

Chatlos, John Calvin. "A Framework of Spirituality for the Future of Naturalism." *Zygon: Journal of Religion and Science* 56, no. 2 (June 2021): 308–34. https://doi.org/10.1111/zygo.12670. Reprinted with permission.

Glasser, William. *Choice Theory: A New Psychology of Personal Freedom*. New York: HarperPerennial, 1998.

Pontin, Jason. "The Importance of Feelings." *MIT Technology Review*, June 17, 2014. https://www.technologyreview.com/2014/06/17/172310/the-importance-of-feelings/.

Rutledge, Gail. "Got Boundaries?" *Visions Journal* 15, no. 1 (2019): 37–39. https://www.heretohelp.bc.ca/sites/default/files/visions-supporting-adult-children-vol15.pdf.

Shapiro, Shauna L., Linda E. Carlson, John A. Astin, and Benedict Freedman. "Mechanisms of Mindfulness." *Journal of Clinical Psychology* 62, no. 3 (March 2006): 373–86. https://doi.org/10.1002/jclp.20237. Reprinted with permission.

CHAPTER 6

CFI Team. "SMART Goals." CFI. Last modified March 23,
2023. https://corporatefinanceinstitute.com/resources/
management/smart-goal/.

Cleveland Clinic. "Autonomic Nervous System." Last reviewed
June 15, 2022. https://my.clevelandclinic.org/health/
body/23273-autonomic-nervous-system.

Ho, Grace. "More Dual-Income Couples in S'pore with Equal
Qualifications: Population Census." *The Straits Times*, June
18, 2021. https://www.straitstimes.com/singapore/politics/
more-dual-income-couples-in-spore-with-equal-qualifica-
tions-population-census.

Porges, Stephen W. "Polyvagal Theory: A Science of Safety."
Frontiers in Integrative Neuroscience 16 (May 2022). https://doi.
org/10.3389/fnint.2022.871227.

CONCLUSION

The Diamond Approach. "Quotes about Essence." Glossary of
Spiritual Wisdom. Accessed April 18, 2023. https://www.dia-
mondapproach.org/glossary/refinery_phrases/essence.

Maxwell, John C. *The Power of Significance: How Purpose Changes
Your Life*. New York: Center Street, 2017.

Tolle, Eckhart. "Eckhart Tolle Special Live Teaching | Conscious
Manifestation." Eckhart Tolle. June 20, 2020. YouTube video.
1:23:40. https://www.youtube.com/watch?v=8G46F9ye204.

ACKNOWLEDGMENTS

This book, *Parenting Unchained*, sparked from a little magical touch from my daughter, Ally, when she was two months old during a late-night breastfeeding. Without this awakened moment reflecting what unconditional love is truly about, I would not be able to be unchained from my past, freeing myself from my inner wounds created from my own interpretation of my upbringing and being aware of my preconception about love and life. Thank you, Ally.

I would also like to thank my husband, Ivan, for giving me the space and freedom to create my life expression through writing this book—through being a parenting coach, through raising my daughter, and through dancing and connecting my mind-body-soul.

I am grateful for my parents, Michael and Juliet, who have raised the five of us as best they could. My grandparents are

Chinese immigrants in Malaysia; my parents are the first genera-
tion of Chinese Malaysians. When they were young, they were living in less than conducive conditions, working very hard to thrive.
Because they did not have a chance to attain sufficient education,
they found they had limited resources available for them to succeed in life. Hence, to be able to send their children to complete
universities is the proudest thing they have done in life, and to
ensure we have a better future, so that life can be easier for us.

I would be less courageous to come this far without the com-
panionship of my siblings, Annie, Anne, Jane, and Boon. Thank
you so much for being there for me, being my most sincere audience, and giving me the feedback I needed to hear. Thanks to
all my nephews and nieces—Javier Tan, Nils Peeters, Athan Lau,
Joven Tan, Avery Lau, Finn Peeters, Nelle Peeters—who add joy
to my life. Some of them are even my social media followers.

I have learned to embrace diverse family backgrounds through
my in-laws. The interactions with my father-in-law, Patrick, and
my mother-in-law, Alice, taught me a great deal about how much
growth I needed in order to accept my imperfections.

To my first teacher in family education, Dr. Susan Walker—
thank you for opening the door for me to discover family education. Pursuing an MEd in family education while setting up a
social enterprise and taking care of my two-year-old in 2012 was
not an easy time for me. However, that journey has given me
hope to pursue my life's purpose.

I have been drawn to dancing or body movement since I was
eleven. I joined a dance club and a dance society in primary

and secondary schools. To be able to dance again after having my daughter has always been at the back of my mind. I found Wu Tao Dance Therapy via a Google search in 2019. I am now a certified Wu Tao Dance Therapy instructor. Dance therapy is an alternative way to connect with ourselves, or another meaningful way to spend time with ourselves. Through dance movements, music, and meditation, our body may send us some messages for us to pay attention to. These messages could surface through practices of observing our body and our internal dialogues. Our body could try to tell us it is time to heal or it is time to take action, etc. I would like to thank Michelle Locke, the founder of Wu Tao Dance International, for creating such a beautiful way to help us reconnect and listen to our body, care for ourselves, and maintain our inner harmony physically, emotionally, and spiritually.

Triple Gs to Anne Ng as I looped her in during the creation of this book: so *great* to have Anne to complete the thoughtful and beautiful book cover and interior illustrations. So *glad* that she did not just take instructions; she asked questions and probed further, allowing me to have more clarity of my ideas about the illustrations. So *grateful* for her suggestions. I always enjoyed the discussions with Anne and found myself learning a little more about the work and myself at the end of each discussion. I highly recommend her should you need an illustrator and/or a graphic designer.

I appreciate the Scribe team who went the extra mile and supported me to complete this book. Special thanks to Sophie

May, the publishing manager who has been supportive and warm; Skyler Gray, who has cocreated this amazing book title; Amanda Woodard, Nicole Jobe, Skylar Griego, Robyn Evans, Braxton Benes, and the editorial and graphic teams, who have given lots of thoughtful and wise suggestions during manuscript editing; and Amy King for her book cover advice and adaptation.

Finally, I would like to express my gratitude toward generous people who helped me unveil my true self. Because of you I can be who I am today and be comfortable in my own skin: Dr. Shefali Tsabary (mentioned in chapters of this book), Sola, Francesca Redden, and Janet Philbin. Furthermore, I am grateful for our paths to have crossed; your care and trust in me has given me strength to keep going and growing: Angela Wee, Tan Chade-Meng, Christine Ryan, Charlotte Ong, Elynn Lorimer, Evelyn Khong, Heather Cline, Josephine Teo, Jimbo Clark, Dr. Lindsay Gibson, Gulcin Bakkaloglu, Alvina Chu, Anne Ng, Chang Bai, Eve Cher, Li Xin, Wong Siew May, Tong Xin, Alma Zhou, Glynda Zhangxi, Nur Kamilah, June Tangsakul, Suzairfisya Sonario, Boon Hwang, Amy Hwang, Karen Hwang, Aow Kim Lian, Spring Fong, Yvonne Chan, Yoko Kawauchi, Ray Goh, Ng Eng Yee, Jade Hong, Roy Sim, James Pang, Ho Chee Kong, Loh Wye Boon, Henry Yap, Ng Kok Chai, Derek Loh, Chow Chee Kiat, Steve (met at UNLV 1994–96), Craig Pozzi (met at PSU 1993), and friends.

As I uncover my inner truth moment by moment with your intersection along my growing journey, I am and will be a more conscious human being, mother, daughter, and wife, and a more passionate and compassionate coach, dance therapy instructor, and educator.

ABOUT THE AUTHOR

Born in Malaysia, Jenny Ng was named by her uncle, the most educated of his eleven siblings, because he thought it would be easy for others to remember. Her surname Ng (pronounced "Ung") originated from the Chinese dialect in Hokkien.

When she is not at work, teaching, or conducting coaching or Wu Tao Dance Therapy sessions, she balances time to care for herself, her families, and friends. For self-care, she practices Vipassana meditation and journaling daily mornings, dances three-minute Wu Tao's wisdom dance during breaks, and goes for nature walks. For family care, she makes sure she eats dinner with her daughter, Ally, daily; has meals with her extended family members regularly; is her husband's good listening ear when he needs it; and holds her family's weekly gratitude practice. She meets up with old and new friends alike over coffee, tea, drinks, and good food. Furthermore, she spends quality time with Ally doing their favorite things, such as cooking, idling, taking photos of flowers and birds, freestyle dancing, imaginative sketching, hot spring hopping, and more.

Jenny lives in Singapore with her husband, Ivan, and her thirteen-year-old daughter, Ally.

CONNECT WITH JENNY

Hi there,

I hope this book, *Parenting Unchained*, has given you an opportunity to engage in some inner dialogues and get curious about how self-parenting may apply to your own self-discovery and personal growth.

You can reach out to me via your preferred online platforms:

- IN: linkedin.com/in/myjennyng
- FB: facebook.com/jenny.jn.ng
- IG: instagram.com/jenny.jn.ng